THE LONG JOURNEY

The Tale of Our Past

By LAURENCE HOUSMAN
Author of "Little Plays of St. Francis," etc.

and C. H. K. MARTEN, M.A.
Vice-Provost of Eton College

WITH ILLUSTRATIONS AND
DRAWINGS FROM MANY SOURCES
AND THREE PICTURES IN COLOUR BY

H. R. MILLAR

BASIL BLACKWELL : OXFORD

First printed August 1933

PRINTED IN GREAT BRITAIN BY
BILLING AND SONS LTD., GUILDFORD AND ESHER

FOREWORD

ALL children love stories. Through these they get their first reading of life in a form which makes life seem so very much worth living. The story may contain things unexpected, causing surprise; but it happens as the child would wish it to happen; it ends—not always happily, but worthily. And because it ends worthily, not making human nature ugly or small, the story has been worth the telling.

History contains many stories which make a similar appeal to the child's mind. They are not all of them happy stories; but they record human worth and human character—truth, courage, adventure, patience, discovery, growth, man in the making. These stories, coming from distant lands and ages, help to enlarge the child's mind, to make him understand that his is not the only country in the world, his not the only race worth thinking about, his not the only time in which great things have been done. In these stories, if wisely chosen, he begins to discover that he is a citizen of the world; that his country has not made itself without the help of other countries; that greatness does not belong only to one race, or wisdom only to the books written in our language.

L. H.
C. H. K. M.

iii

CONTENTS

CONTENTS

ILLUSTRATIONS

COLOUR PLATES

BY

H. R. MILLAR

---

* A coloured illustration may be obtained from the British Museum
for 1s.

ILLUSTRATIONS

PAGE

ILLUSTRATIONS

ILLUSTRATIONS

ILLUSTRATIONS

Besides the statue of the Lohan and the head of Cæsar reproduced in this volume, those visiting the British Museum should see in the Gallery of Casts (in the basement) (i.) Priam begging Achilles for the body of Hector; (ii.) the fragment of a statue of Leonidas set up on his tomb and found in 1925; (iii.) Persian soldiers (227, 228); (iv.) bronze statue of a Charioteer (94). In the Ephesus Room are the heads of Homer, Alexander (1,857), and Socrates.

THE ANCIENT WORLD

THE world is old,
  The years have rolled,
And Rome was not built in a day;
  And go man must—
  Be it mud or dust—
On, on, by the forward way.

In the days forgot,
  When man was not,
At a jog-trot went Time;
  And, go where he will,
  Time stands not still;
There's ever a hill to climb.

But none with a top
  On which to stop—
No place where man may rest;
  As he comes anew
  To the distant view,
There stands a further crest.

Look back, look back,
By the beaten track
Of the past, and its famous story—
To the land God blessed,
And Rome at her best,
And Greece in her days of glory !

And then look ahead:
The past has fled,
But new life is waking.
Reach out your hands
To the cities and lands
Where the world is still a-making.

The story is told,
And the sorrow is old
Of the half-done things, and the undone.
So we'll not wait
For the fall of fate,
But go on with the building of London !

Take courage anew,
For the story's true
How Life has never an ending.
And there's never an ill,
If the heart has will,
Too great for a good man's mending.

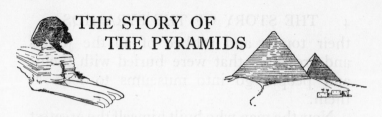

THE STORY OF
THE PYRAMIDS

THE strongest and most lasting buildings in the world are the Pyramids of Egypt. They are nearly five thousand years old. They are too broad to fall down or be blown down, and too big to be pulled down.

These buildings which have lasted so well are tombs; they were built for the burial of the dead. The ancient Egyptians already believed that the soul of man lived on for ever when the body died. On this belief they formed their religion; and out of that came the form of their tombs. The great men of Egypt—the priests and the Kings—wished that after death their bodies should be kept safe from decay. So when any of them died, first his body was preserved in spice and made into a mummy, and then it was put into a strong tomb walled round with rock, so that no one could get at it.

But in spite of all their care a great many of these monuments have since been opened, and the mummies taken out of

their tombs and robbed of all the jewels
and treasures that were buried with them;
and people go into museums to look at
them.

Now the man who built himself the greatest
tomb that has ever been known was Cheops,
King of Egypt. It was he who built the
Great Pyramid, the biggest of all of them;
and he made a place for his body to lie deep
down in the middle of it, so that travellers
going by should point and say, " There lies
Cheops, the mightiest of Kings."

That tomb which he built for himself has
in it more stone than any other building in the
world. It is more than 100 feet higher than
St. Paul's Cathedral; and nearly two-thirds
of a mile round its base. An ancient story
tells us that it was twenty years building;
and all that time a hundred thousand
men were working to get it done. How it
was done nobody knows to this day, for
its stones are of great size and weight; and
they must have had wonderful machines to
drag them all the way from the quarries in
which they were hewn, and to set them up
in their place so many hundred feet above
ground.

THE ENTRANCE TO THE PYRAMID.

HERE IS THE GREAT PYRAMID.

Its height is 150 yards, and the length of the side is 250 yards. Near the three camels is the Sphinx. The Sphinx has the body of a lion and the head of a man; this head is the largest portrait of a king in the world— the face is $13\frac{1}{2}$ feet broad, and the ear is $4\frac{1}{2}$ feet long!

No picture of the machines they used has ever been found; but there are pictures, on stone walls, of slaves working under the whips of their masters at some of the great buildings for which Egypt was famous, and the ruins of which remain to this day.

Nearly all we know of the wonders of ancient Egypt has to come to us from those ruins and the tombs: from stone, and metal, and wall-paintings, and the embalmed bodies of the dead—things which have no life. But, strange to say, other things have lasted which have life in them. In some of the jars placed in tombs, corn grains have been found, and when these are sown in the earth they grow. There they have waited thousands of years, and have not died.

A short while ago a few grains of seed were found in the hand of a dead mummy. And when these were sown they grew into climbing plants and bore bright flowers—like those which we call " morning glories."

All know the story of " The Sleeping Beauty "—the Princess who slept for a hundred years and then woke. That is a fairy story; but this story, of the flower which slept for thousands of years and then woke again, is a true one. It really happened.

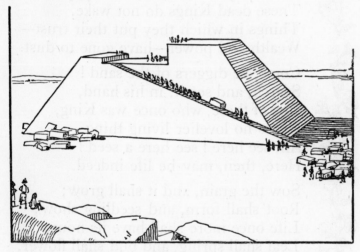

HERE IS THE BUILDING OF A PYRAMID.

You see the inclined ascents up which a stone block is being dragged. These ascents or ramps were built of sun-baked brick, and were removed when the Pyramid was finished.

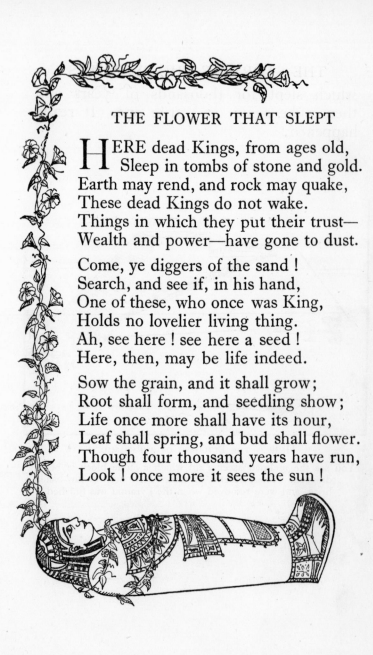

THE FLOWER THAT SLEPT

HERE dead Kings, from ages old,
　　Sleep in tombs of stone and gold.
Earth may rend, and rock may quake,
These dead Kings do not wake.
Things in which they put their trust—
Wealth and power—have gone to dust.

Come, ye diggers of the sand !
Search, and see if, in his hand,
One of these, who once was King,
Holds no lovelier living thing.
Ah, see here ! see here a seed !
Here, then, may be life indeed.

Sow the grain, and it shall grow;
Root shall form, and seedling show;
Life once more shall have its hour,
Leaf shall spring, and bud shall flower.
Though four thousand years have run,
Look ! once more it sees the sun !

THE MAN WHO FOUND PEACE

ABOUT 500 B.C.

GREAT men are not all alike. There have been great men of war, and there have been great men of peace. At the very time when Leonidas and his brave three hundred fought and died to save Greece from the armies of Persia (see page 82) there was living in India a good and a great man, from whose life and teaching came one of the great religions of the world. He was a true man of peace; his name was Gautama Buddha, and this is his story.

His father was an Indian Prince or Rajah.

At his birth the child was named Siddhartha, Gautama being his family name; but to the world ever since he has been known as the Buddha, which means, the man to whom light came.

Born to wealth and rank, he spent his youth in a life of ease and pleasure. His father and those about him were at great pains to keep him from knowing any unpleasant things. He did not know that there

9

were such things in the world as suffering
and poverty and disease; and he had never
heard of death.

When he was nineteen he married a
beautiful maiden, daughter of a neighbouring Rajah. They were very happy together,
spending all their days in amusement and
idleness; and he cared nothing for the affairs
of the country, which some day he would
have to rule; nor did he practise himself in
arms as a warrior; nor did he study books
or learning.

For which reason, we are told, his kinsmen
complained to his father the Rajah, saying
that out of such a life he could not become
a fit ruler.

The story goes that when Gautama heard
this complaint, he challenged his kinsmen
to meet him in any games of strength or skill
they liked to name; also to compete with
him in learning. The challenge was accepted; but when they came to trial he beat
them all; for in body he was very beautiful
and strong, and of high stature, while in
quickness of understanding no one could
equal him.

Some while after this, in his twenty-ninth

year, Gautama one day went riding in his
chariot beyond the carefully kept woods and
pleasure-grounds where hitherto his life had
been spent. On the road he met a poor
ragged man, bent and broken with age.

He had never seen such a sight before, and
he asked his charioteer what it meant. And
Channa, the charioteer, answered: "That
is old age; and we must all come to it at
last."

A few days later he passed, in like manner,
a man suffering from a horrible disease.
And again to his inquiry as to the meaning of
it, Channa answered: "That is sickness;
in some form or other it will take all of
us."

On a third occasion he came upon a dead
body; and when he inquired of its meaning,
Channa replied: "That is death which takes
all living things at the last."

To find such terrible things as these in
the world made Gautama very unhappy;
it seemed to him that, in spite of his present
ease, he was living a doomed life.

But some while after, he passed on the
road a man—in poor clothing, indeed, and
showing the signs of age; but his manner

was noble, and his face calm and serene.
Then he said to Channa, the charioteer:
" There is one who is both poor and old,
yet he seems happy.   How is that possible ?"
And Channa answered: " He is a holy man:
he heeds neither pain nor poverty, and does
not fear death."

Then Gautama said to himself: " If such
things as pain and death must needs be, then
he who fears them not has the true secret of
life, being freed from its fears."

Now that day, as Gautama returned home,
word was brought to him that his wife
had given birth to a son.   As he drew
near, the house was filled with sounds of
rejoicing.   Through the gate came dancing
to meet him a young maiden, who sang:
" Happy is the father !   Happy is the mother !
Happy is the son."

Now, in the language in which she sang,
the word " happy " means also " freed."
And Gautama said to himself: " Is anyone
happy who is not freed from the fear of
suffering and death ?"

Having asked himself that question, he
could not put it out of his mind.   From that
very day he determined that he must go and

discover the true secret of life—how to be free from the fear which men have of the things which they call evil.

He waited till night; then, having kissed his wife and child as they lay asleep, he departed secretly; and putting from him all his goods and belongings, he began wandering from place to place, going as a poor student, without money, without a name, and without a home.

Sometimes he would stop to listen to famous teachers, or talk with their disciples, seeking from one or other to find the true way of life which should lift him above its evils. Sometimes he went apart to desert places, and spent days alone, fasting and praying. Once, a legend tells, he sat down under the shade of a certain tree, and there remained many days, tempted by all the desires of man—the desire for power, for pleasure, for long life, for riches, for fame, for home, wife, and children, and for all the other good things which men wish to possess. And while he thought of them he saw how these things must all end at last and come to nothing. So, in order that he might really be free, he put them out of his heart, together with fear of all the evil things which might also happen to him.

Thus, having conquered desire and conquered fear, he found that only love re-

HERE IS A CHINESE PICTURE OF THE LITTLE BOY OFFERING TO
  BUDDHA ALL THAT HE HAS, WHICH IS THE DUST HE HAS TO
  PLAY WITH.

To the left you see Buddha and his disciples. Buddha has a
  circle round his head, and in his left hand holds a bowl, into
  which the boy is putting his dust. There is a garden with
  a well and a bridge and children playing games.

mained, and that to love all alike was the real way of life. This was the secret of his teaching. He found it when he was in his thirtieth year, young, strong, and of good fortune, the heir to great possessions. And from that time on, he spent his life teaching it as the true way of peace, giving up all he had for the love and service of his fellow-men.

As he went about teaching, people began to understand and see truth in it; even little children, when he came among them, felt drawn towards him. The story goes that one day he came where a number of them sat playing, making little heaps of dust and pretending that they were houses. And one of the children got up and brought his little house of dust to the great teacher, because he had nothing else to give him. And Gautama accepted it as though it were a gift of great price.

When, after long wandering, he returned to his own city, he took with him a beggar's bowl and went through the streets asking alms. His father, the Rajah, hearing of it, came out in great distress to complain. " Illustrious son," he said, " why do you expose yourself thus to shame ? Am I not willing to give you all that you need ?   Is it right that a son of Kings should go through the streets begging ?"

But Gautama answered: " It is not as a son of Kings, but as a son of the prophets, that I do this.   For the prophets, who owned nothing in this world, had often to beg their bread; and they, in return, received charity, which is of more worth than riches.   See, here in my bowl is charity.   Come and share it with me, for it is a great treasure, and thus only have I found it."

Then, the story goes, the Rajah took the bowl from his son's hand and led him into the house, and shared with him that gift of charity which a life of poverty had brought him.

Also to his wife did Buddha reveal the secret of that true way of life which he had found for himself, free from fear and from vain desires; and she also, though a Princess by birth, chose poverty and became one of his followers.

Thus, by example and teaching, Buddha continued to gather disciples about him, till, at the age of eighty, he died, uttering to his followers words of peace and wisdom.

After his death his teaching became a religion, and passed from India to many other countries in Asia. And to this day it is the faith which, having lasted for over two thousand years, is held by a hundred and fifty million of the human race. Of these more than eleven million live in India, and are our fellow-subjects under the same King.

In nearly all the statues of Buddha that we see, he is shown seated, with his hands and his feet quietly folded, and his eyes shut. For this is the statue of the man who found peace, and who taught that only by peace can man learn wisdom.

THIS IS A PHOTOGRAPH OF A SEATED FIGURE IN COLOURED POTTERY OF ONE OF BUDDHA'S SIXTEEN DISCIPLES.

It was made in China some 1,000 to 1,500 years ago, and is now in the British Museum. The ears are large and the forehead flat—chief of the signs in Chinese art of a holy person.

THE TALE OF TROY

I.—The Wrath of Achilles

MANY years ago, in one of the cities of Greece, lived a most beautiful Queen named Helen. She was so beautiful that Paris, son of Priam, King of Troy, carried her away across the sea to his own city. And all the Princes of Greece went after them to fetch her back again.

But the Trojans were too proud of her beauty to let her go. So the Greeks came in their ships, with a strong host, and laid siege to Troy.

In the war which followed, all the greatest chiefs and warriors of that day fought on one side or the other. On the side of the Greeks was Ulysses, the wise King of Ithaca; and Achilles, who fought so well that men said he could not be wounded. On the side of the Trojans, together with many chiefs from neighbouring cities, were the fifty sons of King Priam, among whom was Hector, the noblest of them all.

Homer, the blind poet, has told the story

18

of that long siege, which lasted for ten years.
Day after day, while the Greeks besieged the
city, the Trojans would come out and fight.
Sometimes the Greeks proved the stronger,
and drove them back again; sometimes the
Trojans fought so well that they drove the
Greeks back to the shore and to their ships.
And all that time fair Queen Helen looked
down from the walls of Troy and saw men
dying for the love and fame of her great
beauty, the Trojans wishing to keep her, and
the Greeks to carry her away.

Now, as often happens when men go to
war, among the Kings and Princes of Greece
there was much quarrelling; and most of all
they quarrelled over the spoil which they took
in battle. One day, over this very thing,
there was a quarrel between Achilles and
another of the Greek Kings named Agamemnon. And because Agamemnon took for
himself something which had belonged to
the other, Achilles went back to his tent in
a rage, and refused to fight any more till
what was his was returned to him.

With Achilles no longer fighting, the
Trojans were stronger than the Greeks; and
so much were they the better that not only

On the right are the Trojans trying to set fire to one of the Greek ships with their torches. On the left is Ajax with his spear defending a Greek ship from the torch-bearers, and behind him his brother is just letting fly an arrow.

did they drive the Greeks back to their ships, but began setting the ships on fire. Only by the great deeds of a warrior named Ajax was the fleet saved from destruction.

But now the Greeks saw how dangerous it was not having Achilles to help them; so they said to Agamemnon: " You must make peace with Achilles, or we shall be beaten."

Agamemnon tried to do so; but Achilles was still too angry to come back and fight himself. But he had a great friend, named Patroclus; and he let Patroclus put on his armour, and take his chariot and horses, and go out to fight in his stead. So wherever Patroclus went through the host, people thought it was Achilles; and the Greeks got their courage back again, while the Trojans lost heart.

But it so happened that, as Patroclus was driving the Trojans before him, he met the great Hector himself, and unable to stand against so great a warrior, by Hector was slain. And the horses of Achilles, standing by, bowed their heads over the body of the dead hero and wept.

When the body of Patroclus was brought back to Achilles, his grief and rage were terrible. Now, to avenge his death, he wished to go back and fight. But Hector had taken from the body the famous armour of Achilles; so he must wait till new armour was made for him. While he waited, the Trojans, having learned that he was still absent, attacked once more; and it seemed as though the Greek camp was about to be taken. Then Achilles rose up in wrath, and though still without armour, went and stood above the trenches and shouted. Three times he shouted, and each time the sound of his shout was so terrible that the Trojans fell back, and the camp was saved.

The next day the new armour of Achilles was ready; putting it on, he went out once more to lead the Greeks into battle. As he came the Trojans fell back before him; but there was only one man now with whom he would fight—Hector, who had slain his dear friend Patroclus.

Up and down he went searching for him, and at last they met. Hector was wearing the arms he had taken from Patroclus; and, as he saw Achilles coming, he turned and ran. For Hector was a great runner, and one of the old Greek ways of fighting was to run first and fight afterwards, so that, when the race was over, the one who had most strength and breath left had the better chance.

Three times round the city ran Hector with Achilles after him; and the Trojans stood on their walls looking on; and the Greeks from their ranks looked on also, to see how this thing would end.

Hector was so swift that Achilles could not catch him; but at last, of his own accord, Hector stopped and turned, and the fight began. It did not take long; the hunger of Achilles for vengeance made him the better man. Hector fell. Dying he begged Achilles to let his body go back to Troy for honourable burial. But Achilles denied his prayer; and as soon as the breath was out of him he fastened the body of Hector to the tail of his chariot, and dragged it away in the dust that he might lay it before the tomb of Patroclus.

Andromache, the dear wife of Hector, looking down from the wall, saw this cruel thing done, and fainted for grief into the arms of her women. Little hope had she then ever to see again the body of her dead lord. But old King Priam had such love for his dead son that, going humbly to the tent of Achilles, he knelt and clasped his knees, and begged that the body might be restored to him.

At first Achilles refused; but after a while the old man's grief touched his heart, and he granted his request. So the body of Hector went back in all honour to be buried by his own people who so loved him, and for whom he had fought so well.

HERE IS ACHILLES IN HIS TWO-HORSED CHARIOT DRAGGING THE BODY OF HECTOR.

II.—The Story of the Wooden Horse

Homer's tale of Troy ends with the death of Hector. But the long weary siege and the fighting still went on. The Trojans had lost their bravest warrior, but the walls of Troy were still unbroken, and the beauty of Helen remained a marvel to men's eyes. In spite of the grief and suffering she had brought on them, the Trojans would not let her go.

Not long after the slaying of Hector, Achilles himself died by the hand of one who was far less noble and brave. Almost by chance an arrow shot by Paris from the city wall struck him in the heel. The great hero (whom it was thought nothing could hurt) died of a slight wound, from which many a man of lesser fame might have recovered. The cause of his death is remembered to this day; for the sinew by which we raise the heel of each foot as we walk is called the " tendon of Achilles," because it was there that Achilles received his death wound.

So day by day the fighting went on, and many heroes on both sides were slain. The

Trojans starved behind their walls; the Greeks wearied for home; but from neither came offer of peace.

Yet in the end it was not by fighting that the city was won. It was the craft of cunning Ulysses which hit on the plan that gave the Greeks victory in such a way as never was done before or since. No other town was ever taken as Troy was taken.

For the Greeks, taught by Ulysses, made a wooden horse of a huge size, the inside of which was hollow; and into it they put as many armed men as it would hold, with a secret door that locked on the inside. Then, leaving their camp and its trenches empty, they embarked with all their spoils of war, and, putting off from shore, rowed out to sea.

The Trojans watched in wonder from their walls till the last of the Greek ships had sailed out of sight. Then, coming out of the city with great joy, they made their way into the deserted camp; and there in its midst they found the wooden horse which the Greeks had left behind. And because of its huge size and strange make, the like of which they had never seen before, they thought it must be something of great worth, sacred to the gods; so, with great labour, they wheeled it into the city, there to be kept as a prize of war.

Night came, and because the Greek ships had all gone, the Trojans set no watch upon their walls, and no sentries at the gates, but went each man in peace to his own home.

But as soon as darkness was upon the sea, the Greek ships turned round again; and very silently, with only the lights of Troy to guide them, rowed back to land. Then the Greek host disembarked, and going under cover of darkness to the appointed place, waited for the signal to be given.

Midnight came. The armed men, hidden in the belly of the wooden horse, unfastened the door, and crept out one by one. Very quietly they stole down to the gate which stood nearest the sea; and when they opened it, there outside were the Greeks all armed and ready, waiting to come in.

Then the word was given; and with a loud shout the whole Greek army rushed the city, killing and destroying as they went.

Thus was the great city of Troy taken. Priam and his sons and all his fighting men were slain, and their women and children carried away captive, to become the slaves of their conquerors.

But beautiful Helen, for whose sake so many Trojans had fought and died, was treated with all honour and respect; and, returning to Greece, she became once more a Queen in her own city; and there lived many years, the most beautiful woman that the world had ever seen.

And now no one can tell the tale of Troy, the great city that went down in flame and ruin after a ten years' siege—the most famous siege in the whole story of man—without telling also of Helen, the beautiful Queen, whose beauty brought Troy to its doom.

THE SONG OF FAIR HELEN

ALL Troy's towers are tumbled down,
　　Helen, Helen, O fair lady !
Stone in dust, and steel in rust,
Wreck has struck the ancient town.
Lives of heroes, victims slain—
Who shall raise them up again,
　　　　Now, fair lady ?

'Twas the wonder of your name,
　　Helen, Helen, O fair lady !
Wrought for Troy that wreck of joy—
Flung her towers to the flame.
If in vain these were not slain,
Who shall raise them up again,
　　　　Now, fair lady ?

By the brightness of your face,
　　Helen, Helen, O fair lady !
Loveliest Queen was ever seen—
From the doom that there took place,
Dark with stain, and stung by pain,
You shall raise them up again,
　　　　O, fair lady !

A WONDERFUL PALACE

THE great hero Ulysses, returning from the siege of Troy, was shipwrecked by storm on the coast of Phæacia.

He had been wandering for ten years; all his companions were dead. Bruised and broken by hardship, without friends, without means, even without clothes, he found himself all alone in a strange land.

He lay down in a wood by the shore, covered himself with leaves to keep warm, and fell asleep.

When he woke he saw a beautiful lady and her maidens running about on the sand, playing at ball.

Ulysses, being a stranger, did not know who the lady was. But she was the Princess Nausicaa, daughter of the King of that land; and she had come with her maidens to wash the clothes of her five brothers, and of the King her father, in a stream which there ran down into the sea. And now, having finished her washing, she was playing games.

Ulysses, seeing the maidens at play, and the clothes lying on the shore, and being greatly in need of help, came out of the wood, and made signs to the lady that he wished to speak with her.

At the first sight of him all her maidens ran away frightened; but the Princess Nausicaa was not afraid. She stood her ground, and waited to hear what the stranger had to say. And when he had told her of his plight, how he was shipwrecked, and homeless, and hungry, she called her maidens back, and bade them give the stranger food and clothing, and oil with which to rub his limbs, after he had washed them in the stream. So the maidens did as she told them, and Ulysses was refreshed, and felt like a man again.

Then the Princess gave orders for the washed linen to be put back into the waggon in which they had brought it to the shore; and, getting into the waggon herself, she drove back home, bidding Ulysses follow her.

Outside the city she left him. And after a time Ulysses followed to the palace of the King, whose name was Alcinöus. As he went he passed fine harbours, and wharfs, and ships full of merchandise; for the Phæacians were a sea-loving people, and all their wealth came to them by sea. He passed under high walls and gateways made strong against the enemy, through streets full of people, till at last he saw shining before him the palace of Alcinöus.

It shone like the sun and moon, for the threshold was of bright bronze, and the walls were of brass; and along the top of the walls was a frieze or border of blue. The door of the palace was gold, and the door-latch was gold; and the door-posts and lintel were silver. On each side of the door, as you entered, were statues of dogs guarding it; some were of gold, and some were of silver. Inside were seats, ranged against the walls from end to end; and over the seats were spread coverings of finely woven linen, the work of women; for these were the seats in which the chiefs sat down to eat and drink when they came to feast in the King's palace.

The chamber was lighted each night by torches, which were held in the hands of gold statues, figures of youths, each standing on a base of its own; and in the hand of each

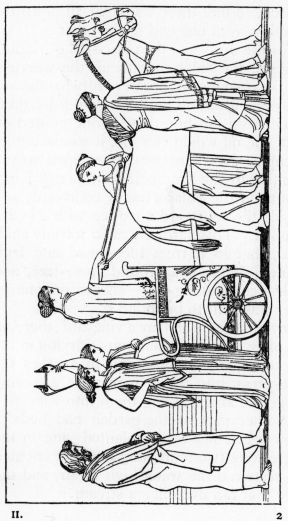

HERE IS NAUSICAA IN HER FAIR WAGGON DRIVING HER TWO MULES, AND ATTENDED BY HER MAIDENS. BEHIND IS ULYSSES.

a torch, so that there was light all down the chamber from one end to the other.

For the service of the palace—the grinding of grain, the baking of bread, the weaving, and the cleaning—there were fifty handmaids always at work. The linen woven by these maidens was so fine that, if one poured oil on it, the oil would run off; it would not go through. Nowhere was finer linen woven than that by the handmaids of this rich King.

Outside the palace was a courtyard, and outside the courtyard a garden with a hedge round it. This garden was so warmly sheltered, that in it trees blossomed and fruit ripened all the year round; pear-tree, and apple-tree, and fig-tree—always on one or other was fruit to be found

Beyond the garden lay a vineyard; there, in one place, could be seen grapes drying in the sun to become raisins, and in another the wine-press, into which men were gathering the grapes and treading them into wine.

Another part of the garden had beds of green vegetables trimly planted; and in the centre were two fountains: one that spouted and scattered the water high in air, and the other that ran deep like a stream.

All these lovely things were to be seen, 3,000 years ago, in or around the palace to which the wandering Ulysses had come to be guest.

So he came into the house; and because the Princess had spoken well of him, the King received him kindly and made him welcome. And when the King had heard the story of his wanderings, he gave him a new ship, with food and water for the journey, and a crew to sail it. So Ulysses, having thanked his kind hosts for all their care and bounty towards him, embarked once more, and set sail for his own land.

THE RETURN OF ULYSSES

I.—The Queen who Waited

WHILE Ulysses, the King of Ithaca, was away at the siege of Troy, his wife Penelope stayed at home and ruled the kingdom. The siege had lasted ten years; then came news that the city had been taken, and that Ulysses was returning home.

Six more years Penelope waited, and he did not come. People began to think that he was dead, and the lesser chiefs and lords of the island said to each other: "This land has no King, and a woman cannot rule alone. Let the Queen take one of us to be her husband, and let him be our new King."

So they all came to the house of Ulysses and told Penelope what they wished her to do. And there in the house they stayed, refusing to go away till she had chosen one of them.

Penelope had with her only her young son, Telemachus, now grown to be a man, and Laertes, the old father of Ulysses, who lived near by. But these two had no power to

prevent the chiefs from doing as they liked;
for the chiefs were many and strong, and had
all their followers about them, ready to do
their bidding. So the chiefs remained in
the house of Ulysses, revelling and feasting;
and whatever they wanted they took without
asking. Day by day there was great waste
of meat and drink; and nothing of all this
did they pay for.

Then Telemachus said to his mother:
" I will go and look for my father. If he is
alive, I will find him and bring him back to
you. If he is dead, I will get word of it."

So Telemachus took ship and sailed away;
and Penelope remained alone.

Now the chiefs wanted Queen Penelope
to choose one of them quickly; but Penelope,
because she loved Ulysses, and believed that
he was still alive, was determined to wait.
So, to gain time, she made a cunning plan,
and she said to the chiefs: " Though my
husband may be dead, his old father lives
still; and according to the custom of this
land, I have a duty to do for him before I can
be free. Let me first weave a shroud for
Laertes to wear in his grave, lest he die
and it be not ready for him. When that is

HERE IS PENELOPE UNWEAVING AT NIGHT THE SHROUD SHE WOVE BY DAY.
On the left are the Chiefs catching her out.

"We saw, as unperceived we took our stand,
The backward labours of her faithless hand."
(Pope's Translation of Homer.)

done, I will choose one of you to be my husband."

So they agreed; and day by day they saw Penelope weaving the shroud. But the weaving never finished; for every night Penelope came secretly and unwove what she had done in the day.

Many days she did this—weeks and months it went on; never before had a shroud taken so long to weave. Then a wicked serving-maid came and told the chiefs what a trick the Queen was playing them; and one night they lay in wait, and caught her; and, very angry at having been deceived so long, they told her she must make up her mind at once. If she did not, they would choose a husband for her, and him she would have to marry, even if it was against her will.

II.—The Dog who knew the Stranger

The chiefs had then been waiting four years, and Ulysses had been wandering for ten. And now, on the very day when this happened, a foreign ship had brought him back to Ithaca.

His son had not found him; he came back

all alone; he had been away twenty years. His clothes were old and tattered, his face was lined with age, his hair was long and beginning to turn grey; nobody meeting him would have guessed that this was the great hero Ulysses, King of Ithaca.

But there were still in that land men who remembered and loved him; and Ulysses, coming by chance to the house of one of these—Eumæus, the swineherd—was received by him as a stranger, and made welcome. And having given him food, Eumæus told the stranger all that had happened in the absence of his dead master, of the shameful things done to his house, and of the danger in which the Queen now stood.

Ulysses, hearing all this, was filled with rage and grief; but he did not yet tell Eumæus who he was, lest word of it should reach the chiefs; for the chiefs hated him and feared his return, and had they known they would have killed him.

But, on the very next day, back came Telemachus, having failed in his search; and there, in the swineherd's hut, his father was waiting for him. As soon as they were alone together, Ulysses revealed himself to his son secretly, and Telemachus, weeping for joy, sprang into his father's arms and kissed him.

Then, from his son also, Ulysses heard tell of the evil deeds done by the chiefs in the house of their absent King; and together they planned vengeance.

Now Telemachus had sent the swineherd to the palace to tell his mother of his return; and soon after, Ulysses and the Prince followed him.

Telemachus, going in first, sent back the swineherd to fetch in the stranger. As they drew near, the two men talked together, and, at the sound of Ulysses' voice, an old sick dog, lying by the gate, raised his head and pricked up his ears. It was the hound Argos, whom, in the days of his youth, Ulysses had trained for the chase. Old, feeble, and dying, the dog, hearing his voice, knew it again; and as Ulysses came near he dropped his ears and wagged his tail, and, looking up into his master's face, he died, happy to have lived to see him once more.

Then, leaning on his staff and clad in rags, King Ulysses entered his own house, where the chiefs sat feasting, and sat down on the threshold like a beggar waiting for alms.

The Dog that Waited

The old dog lies at his master's gate;
    Twenty years he has waited,
Day after day, for the freeing of fate,
    And the sound of a footfall belated.

Many come forth, and many go in,
    And little they pay him notice;
For the dog is mangey, feeble, and thin:
    See how shabby his coat is !

Comes a beggar, all clothed in rags;
    Hark ! the beggar is speaking.
The dog's ears prick, and his old tail wags;
    This is the voice he was seeking !

The beggar halts and over him bends;
    His rags cannot disguise him.
Met again are the parted friends:
    The dog looks up and eyes him.

Thus to his palace returns the King;
    Within lie hate and danger.
A dying dog is the only thing
    Which knows him not for a stranger.

The dog is dead, his bones are dust,
    And poor were his life's wages;
But the story told of his faithful trust
    Has come to us down the ages.

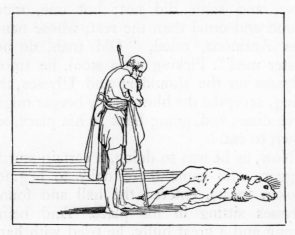

III.—The King who came as a Beggar

Telemachus was sitting at the table where food was being served; and when he saw his father enter, he called Eumæus and bade him take food to the stranger. For no man there, except Telemachus, knew who he was. Then—to test the hearts of the chiefs, and see if they had any kindness—Telemachus told the stranger to go round the table with his wallet and ask for alms.

So Ulysses, the King, went to each in turn, begging bread in his own palace. Some gave, and some did not; but one, more proud and cruel than the rest, whose name was Antinöus, cried, "Old man, do not pester me!" Picking up a stool, he smote Ulysses on the shoulder; and Ulysses, the King, accepted the blow as any beggar might have done, and, going back to his place, sat down to eat.

Now, as he was so doing, a certain sturdy beggar, who came there daily to beg for broken meats, entered the hall and found Ulysses sitting in his place. And being strong and a great bully, he tried with hard words and threats to drive him away.

The chiefs, hearing the big beggar abusing the stranger, called on them to fight it out, little doubting that the bigger and younger one would win.

But as soon as Ulysses stood up and stripped off his rags for the fight, the beggar was afraid and tried to run away; but the chiefs would not let him. So the two were brought face to face, and the fight started. But no sooner was it begun than it ended; for at the first blow given him by Ulysses, the other fell with his jaw broken; and all wondered how a poor old beggar could have such strength.

Presently word of the stranger's coming reached the Queen. So the next day, hearing that he had travelled in far lands, she sent word that she would speak with him, hoping that he might have news of her lost husband.

That night Penelope came down into the hall adorned with jewels and wearing rich raiment, so that the chiefs might think she was of a mind to marry one of them. And because of her great beauty, the chiefs came and made gifts to her, hoping by these to win her favour. But Penelope cared for none of them; she longed only for her dear lord, of whom she now hoped to get news.

So she went and sat down by the fire where, unwashed and in rags, the stranger sat also. And in answer to her questions he told how, in one place and another, he had met Ulysses still living, and on his way home, though his coming had been delayed.

Then, for joy and thankfulness at that news, Penelope bade her old nurse fetch warm water from the caldron and wash the beggar's feet as though he had been an honoured guest. And the nurse did so, and, filling a bowl, began washing not his feet only but his legs also, even to above the knee.

Now in his youth Ulysses had been wounded by a wild boar, and the scar was still on his thigh, and the nurse had seen it of old. So when she saw that scar again, not changed as his face had changed, then at once and for certain she knew him. And letting go his foot, it fell into the bowl, and the water splashed out upon the ground.

Then Ulysses saw that she knew him,

and signed quickly that she must not say a word—not even to the Queen, lest her joy should betray the secret. For if the chiefs knew that this was their King come back again, they would at once rise up and kill him; and what could Ulysses do against so many, having none to help him but his son and the faithful swineherd?

So the old nurse held her tongue, and told nobody; and that night Ulysses and his son made plans together how they should punish the wicked chiefs for all the evil things they had done in their King's absence.

IV.—The Bow of Ulysses

Now Eumæus, the swineherd, had a friend, a herdsman, who also was faithful to the memory of his old master, and longed for his return. And this herdsman, coming with Eumæus to the palace, had seen the stranger, and had felt drawn to him even as Eumæus had been, though neither of them yet knew him.

But now, feeling sure that these two could be trusted, Ulysses showed them the scar; and satisfied by that proof that he was indeed

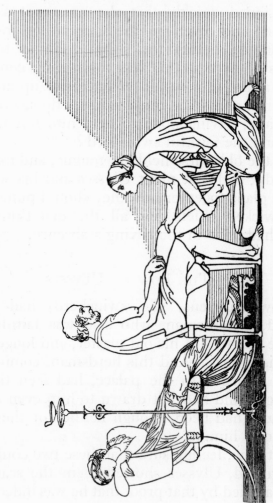

HERE IS THE OLD NURSE SEEING ON THE LEG OF ULYSSES THE SCAR BY WHICH SHE
KNEW HIM. ON THE LEFT IS PENELOPE.

their old master, they promised gladly to do all he asked of them.

Then Ulysses told these two faithful ones and his son of all that he had planned. He said to his son: "Tonight, when the chiefs are a-bed, go down into the hall, and take from the walls all the spears and shields which hang there, and hide them. And if tomorrow any ask for them, then say that they have gone to be cleaned because the smoke of the torches has blackened them." And Telemachus did as his wise father had told him.

Then said Ulysses to his old nurse: "Tomorrow, when the chiefs sit down to feast, send the womenfolk into their chambers and shut all doors fast. And whatever you hear then of uproar and shouting, let none come forth till I give command. So shall the will of Heaven be done."

Then he said to Eumæus and his friend the herdsman: "Tomorrow, when the chiefs are feasting, go forth from the hall and bar up the doors, and see that ye make all fast, so that none seeking escape may go out, and none seeking to bring help may come in."

So did the wise Ulysses cunningly devise

that the great hall of his palace should be made a trap for his enemies.

Now of all this Penelope knew nothing; and she had promised that on the morrow she would at last choose one of the chiefs to be her husband. So, on the evening of the next day, when the chiefs had returned from the chase, Penelope came down into the hall, bearing in her hand the great bow of Ulysses and a quiver full of arrows. And she said to the chiefs: " Now will I make my choice. See, here is the bow of Ulysses, which no hand but his has ever strung, nor loosed from it an arrow. To him who shall most easily string this bow, and send an arrow to the mark, I will give myself in marriage."

Then, one after another, the chiefs took the bow, and tried to string it, but could not; even Antinöus, the strongest and the most boastful, could not bend it to notch the string to its place.

Telemachus tried also; but because he was young and had not reached his full strength, he too failed like the others.

Then said Antinöus, speaking for the rest: " Let this wait till another day, for now we

PENELOPE WITH THE BOW OF ULYSSES.

are weary from the chase, and our strength
has failed us. Doubtless tomorrow one of
us will do this thing and win the prize."

So, at the bidding of her wise son Telemachus, Penelope left the bow in his hands,
and returned to her own chamber.

And the nurse barred the door after her,
as Ulysses her lord had given command.

V.—THE BENDING OF THE BOW

Then Prince Telemachus stood up on the
high dais, holding the bow of his father,
and looking down on the chiefs, where they
sat feasting below, he saw them verily as
men already dead, for the doom of Heaven
was now on them.

Then did the stranger, that was Ulysses,
rise up from his seat in the lower hall, and
give to Eumæus and the herdsman the
signal for which they had waited. And going
forth they barred the doors, making them so
fast that none might go in or out.

Meanwhile Ulysses spake to the chiefs,
and said: " I, too, will make trial of this
bow, for when I was young I had strength,
and some of it is still left to me."

Then the chiefs, because they feared to be beaten by an old beggar, cried out, forbidding him. But Telemachus said: "This bow of my father's is now mine, and I will give it to whom I please. What right have any of you to say no?"

So Ulysses came and stood by his son upon the high dais, and the doomed chiefs all sat below and watched, not knowing that their end was at hand.

Then Ulysses set the bow against his knee, and notched the string easily, and taking an arrow, he shot it to the mark at the far end of the hall. All the air of the hall whistled as it went, and it struck the middle of the mark straight and true, and, as it struck, over the roof of the hall the Heavens thundered.

"Now will we have other sport!" cried Ulysses; and at that word, Telemachus ran swiftly and armed himself, and came and stood at his father's side—they two against all the rest.

Then the great Ulysses stripped off his rags, and showed himself the man he was, wrathful, and strong, and terrible. And he cried in a loud voice: "Now shall the gods give me strength for a greater deed; and lo, my mark is before me. For I am Ulysses, whose house ye have defiled, and whose wife ye sought to take from me !" So saying, he notched an arrow and let it go, and the arrow flew and struck Antinöus in the throat as he was drinking. The wine-cup dropped from his hand, and he fell dead.

Then all the chiefs sprang up from the feast in fear, and some ran seeking to escape, but the doors were barred; and others sought weapons, but the spears and shields were gone, and they had nothing but their short swords left to them. But against the arrows of Ulysses, and the long spear of Telemachus, these were of small avail; for as fast as they strove to climb on to the high dais Telemachus thrust them down again. And even as they strove, the arrows of Ulysses flew, and in every arrow that he sent there was death.

So the slaying went on till all were dead; and there was silence and peace once more in the hall of Ulysses.

Then Ulysses went and made himself known to his faithful wife Penelope, who, though first doubting the truth, received him at last into her arms with great joy and thankfulness.

Also to Laertes, old and feeble and near his end, he came to receive at his hands a father's blessing.

Thus did Ulysses return to his own house and people after twenty years, to become once more King of Ithaca.

PENELOPE CARRYING THE BOW OF ULYSSES TO THE
SUITORS.

THE LORD OF THE BOW

In the hall of the Palace the Chiefs sit feasting. ULYSSES, *disguised as a beggar, sits alone by the hearth.* TELEMACHUS, *his son, stands near him.* QUEEN PENELOPE *enters, followed by two of her maidens. She bears in her hand the bow of* ULYSSES. *One of the maidens carries a quiver of arrows.*

PENELOPE.

Ye men of might, and chieftains of this land
Which lacks its lord—suitors, at whose command,
I, a King's widow, here must make my choice,
And, all unwilling, wed again—now hear,
Ere yet I yield consent, hear ye the voice
(Ye, that are strong) of a weak woman's prayer !

FIRST CHIEF.

Aye, speak, and we will hearken ! Should we find
Good reason in it, we shall be well inclined
To grant it. Speak !

PENELOPE.   Behold, then, here I stand,
Holding unbent—lacking its master's hand—
This bow of him whom once I called my
   lord.
See, how unnotched and slack now hangs
   the cord,
And in the quiver how the arrows hide
Their bright stained feathers. I will be his
   bride
Who best shall bend this bow; and him
   alone.
Lord of the bow, I, for my lord, will own,
Serve, love, obey. Surely this test shall tell
One man's true worth. How say ye? Is
   it well?

FIRST CHIEF.
O subtle woman! Is it strength we lack?
Now shame on him who from this task
   turns back!
What say ye, lords? Are we not all agreed?

CHIEFS.   All, all! We are!

FIRST CHIEF.   Come, then, put
   back with speed
Benches and board; make clear the central
   hall,

Set up a target against yonder wall,
Then take your turns; and, be it lose or win,
Hands to the challenge!

CHIEFS.   Aye! Begin! Begin!

PENELOPE.

So be it! Take the bow! But, if ye fail,
For none of you will I put off my veil
Of widowhood. For though my lord be
    dead,
No man less worthy shall have me to wed.

[*Meanwhile the servants have cleared the hall,
    and have set up a target at the far end.*
    TELEMACHUS *takes the bow from the
    Queen's hand.*]

TELEMACHUS.

Now all is ready. Come, my lords, and
    show
Which of you best can bend my father's
    bow.

[*The* FIRST CHIEF *takes the bow, and tries to
    bend it. The others look on, and laugh.*]

SECOND CHIEF.

Ah, ha! He cannot do it! I had a doubt.

THIRD CHIEF.

Try it again! The other way about!

FOURTH CHIEF. Heads, tails, he cannot!

SECOND CHIEF.
> Give it to me !   Here, fellows, stand away !
> You wait your turn !   Give me more room,
>   I say.

FOURTH CHIEF.
> More room ?   More rope—a longer bit of
>   string
> Is what *you* want !

SECOND CHIEF.   One cannot bend the thing !
> 'Tis iron, not wood !
> [*They all laugh at him.*]
>   You laugh !   Does any man
> Think he'll do better ?   Let him laugh who
>   can !
> Come, joker, take *your* turn !
> [*The* FOURTH CHIEF *tries, and fails.*]
>   He jokes no more !

THIRD CHIEF.
> Come, now let *me* try.   [*He tries and fails.*]

TELEMACHUS.   Ye have failed, all four.
> Now, are there others ?

FIFTH CHIEF.   Pah !   This is no test.
> Men after supper can't be at their best.
> We've ate and drunk too much.   Therefore,
>   I say
> Let's leave this matter till another day.

Tomorrow early, after rise of sun,
When we're well rested, you shall see it
  done.

PENELOPE.
  Until tomorrow, then, you leave me free ?
  Good-night, my lords, sleep well.
  [PENELOPE *and her maidens retire.* ULYSSES
    *rises from the hearth and advances towards
    the* CHIEFS.]

ULYSSES.   Give it to me.

FIRST CHIEF (*astonished*). Give *what* to you ?

ULYSSES.   The bow.

FIRST CHIEF.   Give *you* the bow ?

THIRD CHIEF. What means the beggar ?

ULYSSES.   I would only know
  If this old hand, which once had strength
    and skill,
  Hath in it of past use some memory still.
  For once I, too, could wrestle and could race,
  And often then was foremost in the chase,
  And from my bow, with many a shaft, I slew
  The flying prey.

FIRST CHIEF.   Art thou a suitor, too,
  For the Queen's hand ? Eh ? What ? Dost
    dare to match

Thy strength of arm 'gainst ours, old cab-
    bage patch ?
Back to thy kennel, beggar !

TELEMACHUS.   Nay, not so.
Ye have not yet mastered my father's bow
Enough to say who shall or shall try
The bending of it. Be he low or high,
Any is welcome. Therefore, to this test
Come on, old man ! And, if you prove the
    best,
From these great lords to you shall go the
    prize.

[ULYSSES *takes the bow from his son's hand,
    and goes up the hall. He mounts the
    steps of the dais.* TELEMACHUS *follows
    him.* ULYSSES *strips off his beggar's rags,
    bends the bow, and notches the string.*]

SECOND CHIEF.
Ha ! He strips well ! Look you, a man of
    size,
Of brawn and muscle. Beggar though he be,
He'd be your match, Antinöus.

FIRST CHIEF.   We'll see !
ULYSSES. Aye, see !
CHIEFS.   Look, look ! The beggar
    has bent the bow !

THIRD CHIEF.

Ye gods! Oh, yonder is a face I know!

ULYSSES.

Ye know me now? Ye know me now too
  late!
The doom of Heaven is on you, and the fate
The gods have willed. Now look your last
  on light;
For here is death, and on your eyes comes
  night!
Thunder, ye gods! and let your heavens be
  dark
Over these men, on whom, set up for mark,
I bend my bow—and smite till all be dust!
[*There is loud thunder, the hall darkens.
  From the darkness come sounds of con-
  fused movement, shouting and cries. They
  cease. There is silence for a while.
  Light returns. All the* CHIEFS *lie dead.*
  ULYSSES *stands and looks down on them
  from the high dais.*]
So they are dead; and all their pride and lust
Are gone like shadows from a sunlit wall!
The wicked shall not thrive: the gods are
  just;
The price is paid; and peace dwells in my hall.

CRŒSUS, THE RICH
(Reigned 568 to 554 b.c.)

I

CRŒSUS, the King of Lydia, was wonderfully rich and wonderfully fortunate. When he began to reign, all his wars were victorious, and he had more gold and treasure than he knew what to do with.

One day, when at the height of his fame and glory, he received a visit from old Solon, the wise law-giver of Athens. Taking Solon into his great treasure-house at Sardis, Crœsus showed him all the wealth of gold and jewels which lay stored there. And when Solon had seen all these things, and the beauty of his palace and the prosperity of his people, the King said to Solon: " Who, of all the men you have ever met or heard of, would you call the happiest ?"

Solon answered: " The happiest I know of was Tellus, the Athenian." Crœsus, who had never heard of him, was much astonished. " Why was he the happiest ?" he asked.

" Because," said Solon, " while he lived his country prospered; he was beautiful and good, he was happy in his children, he was happy in his own life; and he died, fighting gloriously for his country, in the hour of victory."

Then Crœsus said: " And after him, what man would you call the most happy ?" For, this time, he thought surely that Solon would name him.

But Solon answered: " Two noble youths, men of Argos, who, when the oxen did not come in time to take their mother to the festival, harnessed themselves to her chariot and drew her to the temple, which was six miles away. Then, for what they had done, their mother, the priestess, prayed that the gods would send them blessing. And that night they lay down to sleep in the temple; and in their sleep they died. These two I count happy."

Then Crœsus was angry, and said: " Why dost thou set the happiness of these common men higher than mine, who am a King favoured of the gods ? Does such fortune as mine seem nought to thee ?"

But Solon answered: " Life is full of

accidents, and a man may live seventy years; and, early or late, trouble may come to him. I count no man happy till he is dead."

Now this answer pleased Crœsus so little that he regarded Solon as a fool, and let him go from the city without honour or reward. Yet in the life of Crœsus, before he died, those words of Solon came true.

II

For first there came to him great grief in the death of his best and favourite son, whose name was Atys, and whom he loved better than his own life. One night the King dreamed a dream; and in his dream he saw his son lying dead—slain by a weapon of iron. So because of this dream he would not let his son go to war; and all spears and javelins were removed out of his reach, and from the walls of his chamber, lest one of them might fall and strike him.

Then there came to the King's court a man named Adrastus, who by accident had killed his own brother, and for that reason had been driven into exile. And because he was without guilt in the matter, Crœsus befriended him, and let him stay as his guest.

And Adrastus and Atys, the King's son, became friends.

Now it chanced at that time that the country was being ravaged by a wild boar of monstrous size, so savage and strong that none had been able to kill it. So the two friends asked leave of the King to go out with a body of picked huntsmen, and slay the monster which was doing such damage.

At first the King, fearing for his son's life, would not consent. But his son said: " What have I to fear, father ? For though the beast is strong and savage, its tusks are bone, not iron. And it is not bone, but iron, that your dream has made you afraid of."

So the King Crœsus let his son go to the hunt, bidding his friend Adrastus watch over him and guard him from all danger.

Now when the two youths and their band of huntsmen had come to the place where the wild boar lay hidden, they surrounded it on all sides with men and dogs; and as the boar rushed out, the huntsmen hurled their spears at him, and the spear of Adrastus, missing the boar, struck Atys, wounding him to death.

II.

3

So word of the death of Atys went back to the King; and presently came the huntsmen carrying the dead body, and with them Adrastus the man he had befriended, who was the cause of his son's death.

Adrastus came and stood before the King, and stretched out his arms, begging that he might be slain as a sacrifice upon the body of his friend. But Crœsus was too noble to seek vengeance on a guiltless man; and with pity, not wrath, he let the slayer of his son go free, forgiving him for what he had done.

But Adrastus would not forgive himself. Too noble to wish to live after having killed his friend, he waited till the King had buried the Prince with all honour. Then going to the tomb alone, he lay down on it, and of his own will died of grief.

For the loss of his son Crœsus mourned two whole years; nor after that did he ever think himself the happiest of men.

III

A few years later another misfortune fell on him. Crœsus, wishing to add another kingdom to his conquests, made war on Cyrus, King of Persia. But Cyrus proved

THIS IS AN OLD GREEK VASE, MADE LESS THAN FIFTY YEARS AFTER
THE DEFEAT OF CRŒSUS.

This picture shows another version of the story according to which
Crœsus, after his defeat, heroically ordered his own pyre to
be built and his slave to light it.

himself the better man. Defeating the
Lydians in the plain before Sardis, he drove
them into the city, and there besieged them.
In a few weeks the city fell, and Crœsus was
taken prisoner.

In those days captive Kings were often put
to a cruel death. Cyrus gave orders for a
great pile to be made; and Crœsus, bound in
chains, was raised to the top of it, and with
him many others of his own people, condemned to die also. Then, down below, the
fire was lighted, and Crœsus stood waiting
for death.

And as he so waited, Crœsus remembered
the words of Solon, and he cried in a loud
voice: " Ah, Solon, Solon! What thou
saidst to me was true !"

Cyrus, standing by, heard the words, but
could not understand them. So he called
an interpreter and bade him ask Crœsus
who it was that he called on. For a time
Crœsus remained silent, then he told the
interpreter of the words spoken to him
by Solon in his days of glory. And when
the interpreter told Cyrus the tale, the
heart of Cyrus changed and was filled with
pity; and he commanded them to put out

the fire, and take down Crœsus and the
other captives from the pile.

But the flames had taken such hold that
Cyrus's men could not get them under, and
the fire was too fierce for any to climb up
and free the captives from their chains. So
it seemed that though Cyrus now wished to
save them, Crœsus and his companions
would have to die. But suddenly the sky,
which had been clear, darkened; clouds
gathered, and there came a storm of rain in
such torrents that by its help the fire was put
out.

Then Cyrus caused Crœsus to be brought
to him. " For here," he said to himself, " is
one whose life has been saved by Heaven.
If the gods so favour him, why did he become my enemy ?" And when he asked
Crœsus why he had made war on him,
Crœsus answered: " I did as fate made me;
for the oracle told me that if I made war on
you I should destroy a great kingdom; and
I did not know that the kingdom I should
destroy would be my own."

Then Cyrus ordered his fetters to be
taken from him, and made him sit by his
side, treating him with the respect due from

one King to another; while all the courtiers looked on in wonder.

Presently Crœsus saw the Persian soldiers plundering the city, going in and coming out again, laden with spoil. And he said to Cyrus : "What are your soldiers doing there ?" Cyrus answered: "They are plundering your city, and carrying away its riches." "Not my city, nor my riches," replied Crœsus, "for they are mine no more. It is now your wealth that they are taking."

Cyrus was struck by this wise answer. What Crœsus had said was quite true. Now that Cyrus had conquered it, the city of Sardis was his. Why, then, should he allow his own soldiers to plunder it ? He gave orders, and so the city was saved.

After that, Crœsus remained for many years the friend and adviser of Cyrus, his conqueror. But his kingdom was never given back to him. Glory and riches and power had all once been his; no one had seemed more fortunate or more favoured by the gods. But for him Solon's word had come true: "I count no man happy till he is dead."

A CHARIOT RACE

ABOUT 500 B.C.

THE Greeks were a great people for playing games; and, like the English, they also loved horse-racing. But the kind of horse-race they liked best was not with riders on horseback, but with chariots. Each chariot had four horses harnessed abreast; and the driver had no seat, but stood up in the open chariot and balanced himself, while the horses raced round and round the course set for them. At each end of the course was a pillar, round which the chariots had to turn; and when many chariots entered for the same race, getting past each other at that point was very dangerous; and men and horses were often killed.

What it was like has been told us in a Greek play, written by a poet named Sophocles, 2,400 years ago. In the play a

messenger comes running with news of what
has just happened, in a chariot race at Delphi,
to a brave youth named Orestes.

Orestes was the son of Agamemnon, one
of the Kings who fought against Troy. He
had gone to Delphi to try and win the prize
in the games which were held there; he won
the foot-race, and the wrestling, and the
quoit-throwing, and the boxing. In each of
these the judges gave him first place.

On the last day of all came the chariot
race. There were ten chariots taking part;
Orestes was in one of them. The chariots
came out on to the course at sunrise. Everybody had got up early: there was a great
crowd to watch, for this was the biggest and
the hardest race of all. If he won this,
Orestes would be unbeaten, and would be
crowned victor of the games.

The ten chariots drove round the course
for the crowd to look at them. Orestes
came fifth, driving a yoke of four beautiful
mares. They took their stations all in a row
at one end of the course, round which they
must go seven times. Then a trumpet
sounded, and off they went: ten charioteers
all shouting, forty horses all galloping their

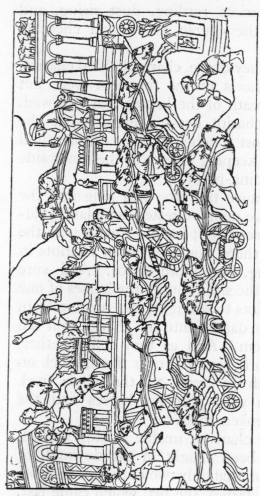

HERE IS A PICTURE OF A CHARIOT RACE IN ANCIENT TIMES.

On the right are the twin pillars round which the chariots are racing. The chariot at the top has already turned and is in the last lap. Two more are racing to turn the pillars; one of them is "cutting in" between his opponent and the wall, and one of his horses has come down. Notice the driver, in the front of the picture, trying to bring the horses round by throwing his whole weight on the reins. In the centre of the picture sits the judge; and on the left are men cheering the racers, and one man on horseback is beating one of the drivers to hurry him on!

hardest, chariots rattling, dust rising, and all round the course the crowd cheering them on.

So close they drove, chariot behind chariot, that the wheels of the foremost were hot with the breath of the horses that followed. So close—chariot beside chariot—that the wheels almost touched as they raced round the course, keeping always to the inner side for the turning-point.

Now because the race was long and the chariots were many, Orestes came last, holding his horses back; for his trust was in the end, when there would be fewer chariots in the running, and more space. And sure enough, in the sixth round, the horses of one of the chariots took fright, and turning from their course, dashed into the chariot that ran next to them. And as they fell together, others from behind fell over them, shock on shock, crash on crash, till the whole track was strewn with plunging horses and the wreck of broken chariots.

So many chariots, unable to stop or turn aside, had been caught in the downfall of the foremost, that only two of the ten chariots which had started, the two which came last, now remained unhurt and able to carry on the race. And these two were the chariot driven by an Athenian and the chariot driven by Orestes.

The Athenian, just in time, had drawn his horses aside from the wreckage, waiting till the way was clear; when close at his heels came Orestes, trying also to pass. And Orestes, seeing that they were the only two left, gave a shout of triumph, and, whipping his horses to full speed, drew along beside him. So, team beside team, they raced which should be first; and sometimes they were level, wheel against wheel, and sometimes one was ahead and sometimes the other.

And now they were on the last round of the race, and the pillar, their last turning-point, was just ahead of them. Orestes was to the fore, and nearest to the pillar; if he could be the first to turn and get past safely the race was his.

But just there he failed. Turning his horses too soon, he struck the pillar with the inner wheel of his chariot. The axle-box broke; off came the wheel; down into the dust went horses, and chariot, and charioteer.

He had lost the race; the Athenian had won.

The messenger bringing that news had seen the wreck of the chariot of Orestes; he had seen the body of the brave youth lifted from the midst of it, bleeding, motionless, without sign of life; he had seen them carry it away. So he had come to bring word that Orestes was dead. But Orestes was not dead; and though he had lost the chariot race, he had won the prize at the games. Afterwards Orestes became famous in Greek history for the doing of things harder and more terrible than the winning of a chariot race. But this story of the race which he rode and lost, though only told in a play, gives us a true picture of what those races were like in old Greek days.

THIS IS A PICTURE FROM A GREEK WATER-POT OF THE DATE OF THIS STORY.

On the right is the turning-point. Here is the leading chariot, and the horse behind has broken away and still races! The second and third chariots are shown on page 71.

HOW ROME LOST A BARGAIN

510 B.C.

TARQUIN, whom men called the Proud, was the last King of ancient Rome. Because of his wickedness and cruelty, the people of Rome drove him out, and would have no more Kings to rule them.

Now had Tarquin known what was going to happen to him he might have become a wiser ruler, and so saved himself and his sons from the fate that presently fell on them. But here is the story of the chance that one day came to him, and of how he missed it.

In those days there were wise women who could foresee the future and were called Sibyls. The Romans held them in great honour; but they did not always know a Sibyl when they saw one. Sometimes a Sibyl did not wish to be known. She came and went; and only afterwards did they find out that she had been among them.

One day an old woman came to the King's court, asking to see him. She would not give her name: she would not say where she came from. But she had nine books, or scrolls, which she offered for sale; and she wanted a high price for them.

A poor-looking creature she was, old and bent; and the price she named was about as much as a King's ransom. Everyone thought she must be mad. Without looking at her books, the King sent her away; he was not going to be troubled by a person of that sort.

The next day she came again. But this time she had only six books. For the six books she asked the same price that she had asked for the nine. This made people laugh; they were more sure than ever that she must be mad. Paying even less heed to the books than before, they sent her away, telling her not to come again.

But the next day she came the third time; and now she brought only three books, and asked the same price for them. Again all the courtiers laughed; but this time the King did not laugh: he asked to see the books. The old woman would not give them up until he had promised to pay her the price she asked for them. And when he had done so, she gave him the three books that remained.

The King opened them, and began turning the pages. "Where are the other books?" he asked: "those that you brought before?" The old woman said: "They were not wanted, so I burned them."

In those books had been written the prophecies of Rome's future greatness, and of all the troubles and perils through which she must pass to become the greatest city of the world. In the three books which remained some of these things were told; but far more had been lost in those which the old woman had burned because they were not wanted.

And so King Tarquin missed knowing the story of his own fate, because, when he had the chance, he would not pay the price for it.

A BRAZIER WITH SCROLL BENEATH.

THE BOOKSELLER

ONCE, in the old days, when Rome was
    in the making—
Ring-a-ding-a-ding-dong ! a many years ago,
There came an old crone, back bent, shaking,
A poor thing, a stranger, whom no one
    seemed to know.

Nine books in hand she bore for sale; but
    no one bought them.
Ring-a-ding-a-ding-dong ! Back they let
    her go.
Back she came the next day; six books she
    brought them.
Named again the same price; again they
    answered " No."

Back she came the third time, with only
    three remaining.
Ring-a-ding-a-ding-dong ! The same price
    still.
This was now the last chance: little use
    complaining.
" Take the books and pay the price, or lose
    them if you will."

The King paid the price, took the books,
    and turned the pages;
(Ring-a-ding-a-ding-dong!) worth their
    weight in gold!
All that here remained—a light for after
    ages—
Prophecy on prophecy, the doom of Rome
    foretold.

" Where are the other books? Oh, folly to
    have spurned them!"
Ring-a-ding-a-ding-dong! Hear the voice
    of fate!
" When I took them back," said the old
    crone, " I burned them.
Then you did not want them; now you are
    too late!"

*   *   *   *   *

Ring-a-ding-a-ding-dong! Through the city
    gate,
Off went the old crone; left him to his fate.

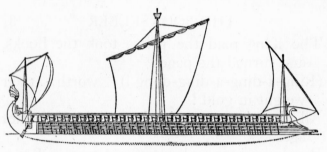

A TRIREME.

THREE HUNDRED BRAVE MEN

480 B.C.

IN the days of ancient Greece there was
a King named Leonidas, than whom no
braver man ever lived. Greece was then
divided into many small city-states, each
with its own King, or ruler; and Leonidas
was King of Sparta.

Now while Leonidas was King, a great
invading army came over from Asia to conquer the whole country and rob the Greeks
of their freedom.

This army, led by Xerxes, King of Persia,
was the greatest that had ever been seen.
It numbered more than two and a half
million men; and besides the army there
was a great fleet of ships. These ships were
called "triremes," because each had in it

" three banks of oars " set one above the other—short oars below and long oars above —with two hundred men to row them.

Wonderful as it was for its numbers, this army was also wonderful in the way of its coming. For King Xerxes caused a great bridge to be built across the Hellespont (which we now call the Dardanelles) from the shore of Asia to the shore of Europe. The bridge was made of a double line of boats fastened together by cables; and over the boats great planks were laid, making a broad road over which the army—foot soldiers, horses, and chariots—marched into Greece.

It is told of this great armed host that the trampling of its feet made roads which lasted for many years, and that where it halted to drink rivers were drained dry, and that what it ate for a single meal brought famine on the people who had to supply it.

Against an army so great and terrible, what hope could there be for the small cities of Greece, which at the most could muster only a few score thousands of men ? And as on land, so at sea—the Persian ships greatly outnumbered the ships of Greece.

Down the coast of Greece came the great army, and the great fleet of Persia with it. As they advanced, tribe after tribe gave in to them, unable to resist. Forced to become allies with the enemy, Greek came to fight against Greek. Thus the army of Persia increased, while the army of Greece grew less.

But when news first came of the danger which threatened, Athens and Sparta, which were the two chief cities of Greece, sent messengers calling on all the others to join them for the defence of their land and liberty. And some, indeed—the people of neighbouring cities—joined and became their allies; but others could not or would not, having already paid tribute to Xerxes and promised to fight for him against their fellow-countrymen.

The Spartans were the strongest Greeks on land, and their army was the bravest; while the Athenians were the strongest by sea. The Spartans and their allies, with Leonidas as leader, marched northward to meet the hosts of Xerxes at the pass of Thermopylæ; while the Greek ships went to Salamis to fight the Persians by sea.

Now Thermopylæ (which means " the gate of the hot springs ") was a place well chosen for defence by few against many; for the pass was narrow, with mountains on either hand, and steep walls of rock to right and to left; and across the narrowest part a wall had been built blocking the way, and behind the wall there was room for an army to shelter.

There, then, Leonidas, with five thousand men, pitched his camp, to await the coming of the Persians, whose numbers were so great that they stretched a three days' journey as they marched. Every day while they waited the Spartans sported and played games, running and wrestling and jumping, so as to keep themselves fit for the battle that lay ahead.

Now Xerxes, hearing that the Greeks had come up into the mountains to meet him, sent out men to spy on them. Soon the spies came back, bringing word how they had seen the Greeks playing games and wrestling; and how afterwards they had sat on the rocks and combed their long hair, as if making ready for a feast.

Then Xerxes, greatly astonished, asked

a Greek captive who was with him what this might mean.

The Greek answered: " These men are preparing themselves for death; for it is the custom of the Spartans, when they know they must die, to adorn their heads with care. Have no doubt, O King, that these men who take death so lightly will sell their lives dearly."

So, indeed, it proved.

The next day, when the forces of Xerxes advanced against the pass in great numbers, not only the Spartans, but their allies also, fought like the sons of gods; and coming out in turns before the wall which barred the pass, they drove back the Persians with great slaughter.

As soon as one body of Greeks was tired of fighting, it withdrew behind the wall, and another body took its place.

So the fight lasted all that day, and the next day also.

Xerxes watched the battle from a throne which had been set up for him on the high ground opposite, and saw how, in so narrow a place, numbers were of little use, and that his army of two millions could not go

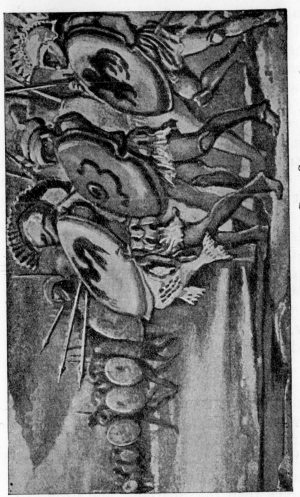

HERE ARE SOME HEAVY-ARMED GREEK SOLDIERS.

Each has a helmet, body and leg armour, and carries a shield (sometimes with pictures of animals, such as serpents, or lions or eagles on it), a spear 6 feet long, and a sword.

forward while these few thousand Greeks stood in their path.

Then was Xerxes in a great strait, and knew not what way to turn for aid; for through that narrow pass, and by no other road, could he advance against the cities of Greece.

But it so chanced that a man of that country, named Ephialtes, knew of a secret track over steep rocks. Up this track men might climb singly, and, descending again, come out on the further side of the pass which the Greeks were defending, and so take them in the rear. Hoping for rich reward, he came to Xerxes, and, betraying his countrymen, sold the secret to the enemy.

So that night Xerxes sent out a chosen leader, who had under him ten thousand picked men; and these, with Ephialtes for guide, climbed the track by night, and about dawn came to the summit where the path began to descend again.

Now the Greeks, being natives of the country, knew well of this path; and at a certain point they had set a body of armed men to keep guard over it. But these men, less brave than the Spartans, and little ex-

pecting at that time and place to see so large
a body of the enemy advancing against them,
were seized with sudden fear. They deserted
their post, and fled down to the Greek camp,
bringing news of the disaster which was
about to fall on them. Already the ten
thousand Persians could be seen descending
upon their rear, and preparing to cut off
their retreat.

Now when Leonidas heard this terrible
news, he saw that the battle was lost and
the pass won for the enemy. But the Greek
army of five thousand good men was not
yet taken; its way of escape still lay open.
So he, being commander-in-chief, gave
orders that all his Greek allies should retire
forthwith, and leave him and his Spartans
to carry on the fight alone.

Speedily the thing was done. Just in
time the main force of the Greeks made
its escape southward from the pass; and
Leonidas and his band remained alone.
Behind them were ten thousand of the enemy,
and before them two million; and they
themselves were only three hundred men.

Leonidas chose no longer to wait. It was
useless now to remain behind walls, his rear

having been taken; so, with his three hundred in solid array of spear and shield, he moved forward against the main army of Xerxes. Wherever he charged, the enemy fell back before him. Behind them their captains, armed with whips, drove them forward again. The barbarians fought unwillingly, and numbers of them were slain; many, as they pressed this way and that, seeking to escape the onslaught of the Spartans, fell and were trampled to death. Before the fight was over, the three hundred had killed thousands.

But gradually the long spears of the Spartans were all broken, and they had only their swords left. So at last numbers began to tell.

Leonidas fell fighting bravely, foremost to the last. Then all the Spartans who remained gathered themselves close into one body, and, standing back to back, fought round their dead leader till not one of them was left.

Thus was the pass won, and Xerxes marched on to the conquest of Greece.

He took and burned Athens, and many other cities. But these victories did not win him the war; for, near by, in a great battle at Salamis, the Greek fleet beat the Persian, almost destroying it; and so the Greeks became masters of the sea.

Xerxes, hearing of this, and fearing that the Greeks might destroy his bridge of boats across the Hellespont, hastened back to his own land with the larger part of his army, and left one of his generals in his place to carry on the conquest of Greece.

But the thing was never done. After much fighting and wasteful war, the Greeks broke the power of the Persians and drove them back to their own land.

Had Persia then been able to conquer Greece, the history of the world would have been changed.   For after that came the great Grecian Age, with its buildings and statues and poems, and the works of its great teachers, from which came wisdom to the world.   All these good things were made possible because the Greeks had remained a free people.

At the entrance to the pass of Thermo-pylæ, on the very spot where they fell, the Greeks buried Leonidas and his three hundred Spartans with great honour.   On the mound over their grave was set up a stone, and on it (because the name Leonidas means lion) the figure of a great lion was carved. And underneath, as a voice speaking for the dead, were these words:

" Go, Stranger, and to holy Sparta tell
    That here, obedient to her word, we
    fell."

A PERSIAN CAVALRYMAN.

KINGS OF TIME

H ITHER, and set ear to ground !
Under earth a rumbling sound
Of far-off thunder shakes the fen.
What comes yonder ? Tell us, then !
'Tis no thunder,
Rolling under,
Sends through earth that sound of wonder;
But the heavy-armoured tramping,
From their last place of encamping,
On the march, of Xerxes' men.

Hark ! a rustling stirs the air,
Sharp as hail. Say, what is there ?
Is it wind with sleety breath,
Or the loud-winged bird of death ?
Whence this rumour ? Tell us right !
'Tis not sleeting,
Nor wings beating,
Sends through air that rumour fleeting :
'Tis, with rattling through the ranks
Of the swords upon their flanks—
Xerxes' men, arrayed for fight !

Gloom upon the morning's glow,
Comes a swift cloud, flying low,

Thick as dust-storm, dark as night:
What is that which strikes on sight ?
       Not cloud drifting,
       Nor sand shifting;
But from ranks of bowmen, lifting
Bows in rows, and bow-string straining,
Lo, a black rain upward raining—
Flocks of arrows loosed for flight.

What is here beneath this mound,
Raised from the deep-furrowed ground ?
Is it grain, or is it grass,
That the season brings to pass ?
What lies under ? Tell us true !
       Here in keeping,
       Not for reaping,
Lovers of their land lie sleeping.
These, the men who feared no thunder:
Life, not death, has ploughed them under,
Kings of Time, a whole world's wonder—
Spartans, whom the Persians slew !

THE WISDOM OF SOCRATES

469-399 B.C.

FOUR hundred years before Christ there lived in Athens a man who was wiser than Solomon, and his name was Socrates. He was very plain to look at; he was very strong; he was fond of a joke. He lived quite simply: he could bear heat and cold without complaint, could walk long distances without tiring, could meet insult without losing his temper, could stand up to an enemy without hatred, could own himself in the wrong without shame.

People called him wise, but he himself said that he knew nothing. And yet he was one of the best teachers that the world has known.

He went about asking questions: that was the way he taught people. For he would question and question till he made them find out that, like himself, they knew almost nothing. Yet all the time he was teaching them to know better.

His disciples would come and talk with

him for hours, trying to answer his questions, and asking him hard questions themselves. And because he sent them away so much happier and wiser than when they came, all his disciples loved him.

But there were others who did not love him at all; for Socrates had a way of getting hold of public men who thought much of themselves, and making them talk by question and answer, and by their answers proving to them how foolish they were.

As he often did this to the important men of the city in the hearing of the young, he was charged with corrupting youth—which really meant teaching the young to think for themselves instead of letting their elders think for them. And because Socrates had made his young disciples think new things in a new way, the rulers of Athens at last decided that he was a very dangerous person, and that his teaching must be stopped.

So he was taken up, and brought before a large court of judges. All the elders of the city sat to try him: they charged him with doing harm to the minds of the young by his teaching. The young loved him, but the judges, not being young themselves, found him guilty.

Now the full punishment for a man found guilty of such a charge was death. But they told Socrates that he might plead for some lesser punishment, since none of them really wished to put him to death.

Socrates would not do so. He said they ought to reward him, because he had done his disciples good and not ill. And in his defence he proved himself so much wiser than his judges, that he made them more angry than ever; and instead of banishing him, as they had meant to do, they sentenced him to death.

But nobody really wanted Socrates to die. Even his judges, after they had condemned him, would have been glad to hear that he had escaped; and it would have been quite easy for him to do so.

Some of his friends made a plan for setting him free, and came to him, while he waited in prison, to tell him of it. But Socrates, though he thanked them, refused to do anything against the laws of his country.

" All my life," he said, " the laws have helped and protected me. Is it right for a

II.   4

man only to obey the laws while they please him? Since by law I am condemned to death, I must obey."

So, in spite of the prayers of his friends and the wishes of his judges, Socrates stayed in prison waiting for the day of his death.

When the day arrived, his disciples came to him early, that he might talk to them for the last time. And the subject they asked him to talk about was the question whether there was life after death.

They talked for hours, some saying one thing, some another; some of them believed, but others doubted. Socrates himself believed in a future life, and he gave them the best reasons for it that he could find.

All that long talk between Socrates and his friends on the day of his death was written down by one of his disciples named Plato; and those who wish can still read it.

While they talked the jailer of the prison came in with the cup of hemlock—the poison ordered by the law—which Socrates had to drink. The jailer himself was weeping: he begged Socrates to forgive him for what he must now do.

Socrates not only forgave him but thanked

SOCRATES IN THE MARKET-PLACE OF ATHENS, TALKING AND ARGUING WITH HIS DISCIPLES.

him. Then, while many of his disciples fell to weeping, Socrates, quite cheerfully and without fear, drank off the poison. And in nothing was his goodness and wisdom more clearly shown than in this—that he died as he had lived, fearing nothing, and at peace with all men—even with those who had condemned him to death.

THE HEMLOCK CUP AND THE
WREATH OF FAME.

THE FARMER WHO SAVED A CITY

458 B.C.

WHILE Rome was growing great and strong, it had many enemies; and many times it suffered defeat and was brought near to ruin. But always, when things were at their worst, the Romans found a leader to win fresh victories for them, and save their country from the enemy.

One of these was a farmer who was nicknamed Cincinnatus, because he had curly hair. The name meant " fuzzy-wuzzy," and by that name he has been known in history ever since.

One day five horsemen came riding into Rome, bringing terrible news. The Roman army had been trapped in a narrow valley by a tribe, with whom they were then at war. The enemy had surrounded the Romans; they were starving, they could not get out. If help did not come soon, they must give in.

When the people of Rome heard this

news, they all said that only one man could save them, and that man was Cincinnatus. He had been their leader before; he must lead them again.

But Cincinnatus was no longer in the army; he had gone back to his farm.

Early in the morning messengers came to him from the city; they found him digging

A Roman Wooden Plough in One Piece Drawn by Two Oxen.
From a very old drawing now in Florence.

in his field. They told him the news, and that Rome had sent for him to be the people's leader, and to find some way to save the army.

Cincinnatus left his digging; he put on his toga (the gown worn by Roman citizens), and went back with the messengers to Rome. There he gave orders that all business should cease; the shops were to shut; every man who could fight must arm himself and be ready to march at sunset; and each must bring with him enough food to last him for five days, and twelve strong wooden stakes with their ends made sharp.

The Romans did as he told them; and that same night he and the army, which he had raised in a single day, set out, every man armed with shield and spear, and carrying his bundle of stakes.

It was still dark night when they came to the place where the Roman army had been trapped. Across the head of the valley the enemy lay strongly encamped; and down below, with steep rock on all sides of them, the Romans waited like prisoners. There was no way by which they could get out.

Then Cincinnatus told his men what they must do with their wooden stakes.

Round the enemy's camp they started driving them into the ground, making a thick hedge of them, too strong for a man to break through. And having driven in their stakes, they raised a great shout, telling the Romans in the valley below that help had come for them, and now was the time to fight.

Then, outside the stakes they began digging a trench, stakes and trench together making a barrier which the enemy could not get through.

The other side, roused by the shouting, came running to drive off the attack of this new enemy, who seemed to have sprung from nowhere. In the darkness all was confusion and fear. They could not tell what numbers were against them. Scarcely had they formed their ranks to meet danger in the rear, when the fierce shouting of the Romans from the valley below called them back again. The army they had trapped was fighting to get out.

And so, attacked on two fronts, the enemy found that fortune had turned against them: they were now trapped themselves. When daylight came they saw themselves shut in by a ditch and a palisade too strong for them to break through; for the enemy were guarding it, and now they had double numbers against them.

Unable to force their way out or hold their own, they gave up the fight and threw down their arms. It had only taken Cincinnatus two days to win the war.

The day after he had marched out with his hastily-gathered forces, he marched back leading an enemy's army captive.

Thus he entered Rome in triumph amid the shouts of the citizens; and having done the work they had sent for him to do, he laid arms aside, and going back to his farm went on with the digging of his fields. For, being a good farmer, he liked digging better than fighting; work on the land meant more to him than fame, or riches, or power.

A VERY OLD STATUE OF A ROMAN CITIZEN IN HIS TOGA.
The toga is thrown over the left shoulder, brought across the back, under the right arm, and then back to the left shoulder.

4*

HOW A FLOCK OF GEESE SAVED A CITY

390 B.C.

THREE hundred years and more after the building of Rome, the Gauls came down from the north and took the city. They were a fierce and warlike tribe, big and strong; all other tribes were afraid of them.

At the news of their coming, nearly all the Romans fled away from the city, leaving it empty; and the Gauls marched in through the gates and took it.

But though most of the people had fled, a few still remained. A noble Roman named Manlius, with a body of picked men, went up into the citadel, which was built on a high rock, to defend it, so that the whole of the city might not fall into the hands of the enemy.

Also certain old men, called Senators, proud of their rank and race, refused to run like the rest. They were too old to fight, but they were not afraid. So putting on their togas, or robes of office, they sat

down each in the doorway of his house, and
waited for the Gauls to come.

The Gauls, on entering the city, found the
streets all empty and silent. But presently
they saw, sitting at the doors of their
houses, men like statues, with long flowing
beards and ivory wands, and wearing white
robes with purple borders.

The old men sat so still that at first the
Gauls were afraid; for they seemed more
like gods than mortal men—so still were they,
so calm and fearless.

Then one of the Gauls drew near, and
reached out his hand, and stroked the beard
of one of the old men. And the old man,
angry at being touched, struck the barbarian
with his ivory wand.

The next moment the old man lay dead;
the Gaul had killed him; and before long not
one of the old Senators remained alive.

Then the Gauls went up against the
citadel, or Capitol as it was called, to take
it; but the rock on which it stood was high
and steep, the walls were strong, the gates
were barred; and Manlius and his men were
there ready to defend it to the death.

So, failing to take the Capitol by assault,

the Gauls stayed down below, and laid siege to it. And all the rest of Rome was theirs to do with as they wished.

Now presently those who had fled from Rome wanted to send word to Manlius of the plans they were making to drive the Gauls out of the city; and a young Roman undertook to carry the message. So one night he swam the Tiber, and climbed up the rock by a secret way, and brought word to Manlius of what was intended.

But one of the Gauls, standing sentry below, had seen the way he went; and the sentry told his leader how, up the steepest side of the rock, lay a path that could be climbed. Where one man had gone many could follow; the Gauls were good climbers.

So the next night a strong band of armed men started to climb. The cliff on that side was so steep that, at the top, the Romans had set no sentry to guard it; and the wall was low. Once at the top, the Gauls would be able to enter and take the Capitol; and Manlius and his men would all be slain.

The Gauls had almost reached the top, and the Roman sentries on the other side had not heard them. But in the temple of the

HERE ARE THE GAULS CLIMBING UP ON EACH OTHER'S
BACKS, AND THE GEESE CACKLING THE ALARM.
Notice the statue of the wolf. (See Book I for story.)

Capitol was a flock of geese, sacred to the goddess Juno; and the geese heard the strangers coming, and started to cackle, as is the way of geese at night when they feel that danger is near them.

Manlius, when he heard the geese, knew that something must be the matter. He seized his sword and shield, and shouting for others to follow, rushed to the low wall just in time to see the head of the foremost Gaul coming up from below.

The Gaul was still climbing the steep rock on hands and knees. Manlius caught hold of him and hurled him back. As he fell he bore down those who were behind him. The Romans from above threw down stones and spears on the enemy; they could advance no more, the attack had failed, the Capitol was saved.

The geese continued to cackle long after the danger was over. But from that day they became famous, because their cry of fear in the night had saved Rome.

After that the siege went on for a long time, and Manlius and his men were almost starving. Some say that, in the end, the Gauls agreed to give up the city in return for a large sum of money; others say that a Roman army came against them from outside, and defeated them. But whichever story is true, it is quite certain that the Gauls went back to their own land the way they had come; while the Romans returned to Rome, and rebuilt the city which the enemy had ruined, making it a greater and a stronger place than it had been before.

ALEXANDER THE GREAT

HE DIED BETWEEN THIRTY-TWO AND THIRTY-THREE IN THE YEAR 323 B.C.

PHILIP, the King of Macedon, north of Greece, was offered a horse which nobody could ride. When anyone tried to mount him, the horse kicked and plunged, and bit so furiously that none dare go near him. The King, thinking such a horse to be useless, was about to send him away. But the King's son, Alexander, said: " It is a shame to let such a fine horse go, just because no one is man enough to ride him !"

Alexander was then only a youth. The King said to him: " Do you think you know more about horses than men who have trained them for years ?" Alexander answered: " I think I could handle this horse better than they have done." " And if you cannot ?" said the King. " Then," said Alexander, " I will pay what the horse has cost you. But if I can, then the horse shall be mine." So the King agreed to let his son try.

HERE IS THE TAMING OF THE HORSE.

On the left is a soldier with a javelin and another with bow and arrows.

Then Alexander went forward and took the horse by the bridle, and turned him so that he faced the sun; for Alexander had seen that the horse shied at its own shadow.

Looking the beast in the eyes, the Prince spoke gently to him, and stroked his head softly, till the horse got used to him.

Then, letting his cloak fall to the ground, Alexander sprang lightly to the saddle, and holding a firm rein, but without spur or whip, he kept the horse under control, till it grew quiet and willing to obey him. And when there came no sign of the rage and fury which the horse had shown toward his other riders, then the Prince set off at a swift gallop, and rode him long and hard till he could go no more.

Having thus mastered the horse, he returned unhurt; and his father said to him: "Oh, my son, thou wilt need a larger kingdom than mine; for Macedon will not hold thee!"

It did not take long for the King's word to prove true. A few years later Philip was dead, and Alexander became King. He was then only twenty. In the next twelve years

Alexander conquered so many countries and kingdoms, that he had under his rule the largest empire that the world had known till then. He had conquered Greece, Asia Minor, Persia, and Egypt, and had even reached India. Then, at the age of thirty-two, he died without an heir, and his great empire was divided among his followers.

And, in course of time, most of the countries he had won became subject to the power of Rome.

Alexander was perhaps the greatest general in all history. He also did more than any single man up to his time to make one part of the world known to the other, and this he did by spreading the Greek way of life.

So, all the more, one likes to hear how in early youth he conquered a fierce and un-tamed horse by kindness and understanding. That horse, which he named Bucephalus, became the most famous horse in history. Alexander made it his war charger; it was with him in all his battles. Often it saved his life by its strength and courage; and when, after his great march into India, Bucephalus died by the banks of the Indus,

Alexander built a town to his memory, and called it Bucephala.

Another story of Alexander tells also of his kindness and understanding. In the city of Corinth there lived in those days a strange old man named Diogenes. He was what is called a philosopher, a lover of wisdom, and was too wise for most people to understand.

His wisdom chiefly consisted in trying to find out on how little he could live, and how many things he could do without. To make his body know that he was its master, he set it to do all sorts of painful and uncomfortable tasks, and never complained of anything. He never shaved, or washed, or cut his hair; he had but a few rags for clothing. His only possession was a wooden bowl, out of which he both ate and drank; till one day, seeing a boy drink water from the hollow of his hand, he threw the bowl away; he could do without it.

Legend says that, having no house, he lived in a tub which stood at the temple door to hold refuse. He had once been taken as a slave; and when his captors asked him by what trade he could make himself useful, Diogenes answered: " You had better

DIOGENES IN HIS EARTHENWARE TUB ASKS THE GREAT CONQUEROR ALEXANDER NOT TO STAND BETWEEN HIM AND THE SUN.

sell me to a man who wants a master." A wise man bought him, and set him to educate his children.

Living this kind of life, with no possessions and no comforts, Diogenes claimed to have become wise. Having nothing to lose, he was afraid of nobody; having no wish to

gain anything, he never flattered. He always
told the truth.

So when Alexander, the great conqueror,
came to Corinth, he asked that he might be
taken to see Diogenes, who was one of the
sights of the city. And there sat the wise
Diogenes, the man who wanted nothing; and
there stood the great Alexander, who wanted
the whole world as his own.

The sight of the old man seemed to please
him; he wished to do him a kindness; anything Diogenes chose to ask for he might
have. Alexander put the question: " Is
there anything I can do for you ? " " Yes,"
said Diogenes. " Don't stand between me
and the sun !"

When the great Alexander heard that wise
and honest answer, he was not in the least
offended or angry, for he saw that here was
a man who also had made conquest of the
world, but in a different way. And he went
away saying to those about him: " If I were
not Alexander, I would be Diogenes."

There could not have been at that time
living in the world two men more unlike
each other than Alexander and Diogenes; but
each was great in his own way. Which of

those two was the wiser? Diogenes did not in the least wish that he was Alexander; but Alexander almost wished that he was Diogenes, because Diogenes was contented and wanted nothing.

THE HEAD OF ALEXANDER MADE IN STONE A FEW YEARS AFTER HIS DEATH, AND NOW IN CONSTANTINOPLE.

He is wearing a lion scalp and two horns, one of which can be seen over his ear.

A BRAVE CONSUL

250 B.C.

REGULUS was a Consul of Rome during the time when the people of Rome and of Carthage were at war. It was a long struggle; for over a hundred years war followed war, each nation trying to destroy the other, for in those days no nation wished any other to have power equal to its own.

Now Regulus, being Consul, was commander of the Roman army; and on land and sea he won many victories over the men of Carthage. One of his victories was so great that on his return he was led in triumph through the streets of Rome, an honour which the Romans only gave to their greatest men.

But some years later Regulus was himself defeated and taken prisoner by the men of Carthage; and the Romans, without Regulus to lead them, had to carry on the war as best they could.

For five years Regulus remained a prisoner.

Then the men of Carthage, being defeated by the Romans, sent messengers to Rome to propose peace. Because Regulus had been so long a prisoner they let him go too; but first they made him promise that, if the Romans refused the terms they offered, he would come back to prison again.

No doubt they hoped that Regulus, tired of being a prisoner, would persuade the Romans to make peace on the terms Carthage wished. But Regulus did not think about himself; he thought only of Rome. So when the men of Carthage named their terms, Regulus said they were not good enough; and though the Senate was inclined to accept them, he pleaded so strongly the other way, that at last, on his advice, the terms were rejected.

Regulus would not even agree that Rome and Carthage should exchange prisoners; so, according to his promise, he went back from his own land, to become once more a captive in the hands of the enemy.

The people of Carthage were told what he had done, and how, because of him, a more favourable peace had been rejected. Then their savage anger knew no bounds.

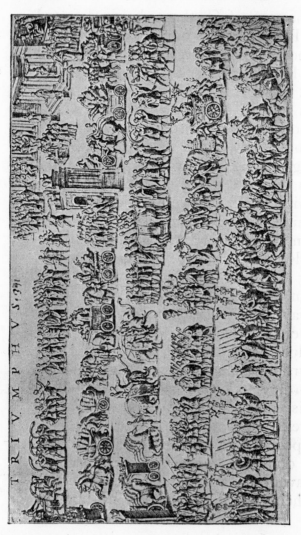

THIS IS A PICTURE OF A ROMAN TRIUMPH SUCH AS REGULUS HAD.

At the head are the chief Roman citizens (see top of picture), followed by trumpeters. Then follow the spoils of war (notice the elephants) and the captives, and the white oxen for the sacrifices. Then come the lictors of the General in red and men burning incense. The General follows in a round chariot drawn by four horses; he carries a laurel bough in his hand, and has a wreath of laurel on his head, above which a slave holds an oak wreath. Behind him come his soldiers.

In revenge they put Regulus to a cruel death.

So died Regulus, the brave Consul, who would not save his own life by allowing anything which he thought not to be for the good of Rome.

THIS WAS THE STANDARD CARRIED BY THE ROMAN ARMIES.

S.P.Q.R.=Senatus Populusque Romanus, that is, " the Senate and the People of Rome."

AN ARMY CROSSES THE ALPS

218 B.C.

HANNIBAL was a very great general. He won many famous victories for the people of Carthage against the Romans, who were then the strongest of all nations.

The people of Carthage and of Rome were at war for a great many years. Rome was in Italy; Carthage was in Africa; but when Hannibal began to fight, his people had already conquered a large part of Spain; and the greatest struggle between Carthage and Rome came when Hannibal led an army from Spain into France, and then across the Alps into Italy.

This is the story of how he crossed the Rhone and the Alps.

He had brought into the south of France— or Gaul as it was then called—an army of 60,000 men of many tribes, and 37 elephants. To reach the Alps he must cross the Rhone, a great and rapid river, defended on its further side by warlike native tribes. How was Hannibal to get across, with his baggage and his elephants, under the darts and spears of a strong enemy ?

This is what he did. He sent part of his army by night twenty-five miles up the river to a place where it was broad and shallow, and the current less swift. There they cut down trees and made rafts big enough to carry the horses; while many of the men made air-bladders of skins, and on the top of the bladders they set their wicker shields, and on these they paddled themselves across.

In this way Hannibal took over a strong force, unknown to the enemy, ready to attack them in the rear when the word was given.

Then Hannibal caused great rafts to be made so big that they looked like islands, on which his elephants might cross. And when the elephants refused to step on to the wooden rafts, he covered them with earth, so that they looked like solid ground. Thus he managed to persuade the elephants to embark on the rafts.

Two days later the force which he had sent up the river made a signal, by means of smoke from beacon fires, that it had reached a point where Hannibal and the rest of the army could cross.

HERE ARE SOME OF HANNIBAL'S ELEPHANTS CROSSING THE RHONE ON RAFTS.

The horses swam the stream, attached by ropes to the boats which carried their riders. Then, suddenly, down came the native tribes to try to stop Hannibal's men from crossing at this point. However, attacked in front and behind, the enemy fled, leaving Hannibal to get the rest of his men across in peace.

The elephants were the chief difficulty, for when they saw themselves being carried out into the water on their island rafts they were terribly frightened; they began to jostle and push and scream, and some of those standing on the edge of the rafts fell off into the river, and had to swim for dear life. But in the end all got safely across. So Hannibal and his army landed, and marched on toward the Alps.

Now the Alps are great mountains which extend range behind range, their tops covered with snow. Winter was coming on; and the passes, which were only foot-tracks, were defended by mountain tribes, ready from the steep slopes above to hurl down rocks on those going below. While the passes were so held, it was impossible to go on.

But Hannibal heard from his guides that the mountaineers only kept guard during the day, and at night returned to their homes. So, to deceive the enemy, who watched all that he did, Hannibal built a great camp, and, when night came on, lighted fires, so that it might seem that the whole army was encamping there for the night. ,But as soon as it was dark, he took with him a strong body of men, lightly armed, and going swiftly through the pass, they climbed up the rocky slopes, and took possession of all the heights which had previously been held by the enemy.

Yet, even so, it was only after a fierce fight, that lasted for nine days, that they came at last to the higher ground which was all covered with snow. And there for two days they rested.

Now many in Hannibal's army came from the hot countries of Africa. They had never seen snow, or felt cold before. And under the snowstorms and icy blasts of the high Alps they suffered terribly; many of the elephants also died, and hundreds of the pack-horses, losing their footing, fell over precipices and were killed.

The suffering and the loss of life were so great that everybody began to despair, all except Hannibal. For now, from the great height they had reached, they could see the plains of Italy below them, rich and warm and populous, a land of oil and corn and wine. And Hannibal, pointing, cried to his followers: "We have only to go down into yonder plain, and conquer the people that dwell there, and we shall be masters of the whole world."

Cheered by the hope of such great reward, they struggled on. But the going down was harder than the coming up: for the way was narrower, and steeper, and more difficult. Storms of snow blinded them as they went; the mountain sides were slippery with ice. They came to a part where the track had been broken away by an avalanche; a new road had to be cut out of the solid rock. Even then, they had often to roll down places too steep for the feet to stand. When at last the plains of Italy were reached a large number of Hannibal's men—over half, according to some historians—had already perished.

Coming south into Italy, he defeated the Romans many times in battle; but still he was unable to break down their brave resistance. In spite of his great victories the wall of Rome was not broken.

5

In due course a Roman army set out to invade Africa, and to save Carthage Hannibal had to return home. There he was beaten by a great Roman general named Scipio. And not many years later he died in exile, by his own hand, so that he might not fall a captive to the Romans.

Hannibal was perhaps the greatest general of ancient times. Had he been able to take Rome after his last battle in Italy, the history of the world would have been changed. But Hannibal failed: Carthage was brought to ruin, and Rome remained the mistress of the ancient world.

THE CAPTIVE CÆSAR

JULIUS CÆSAR. BORN 100 B.C.

THIS is what happened to Julius Cæsar when he was quite a young man, before he had become famous. Going on a sea voyage, he was taken prisoner by pirates; for in those days pirates were many and strong, and had great fleets of ships, and strongholds on islands which they called their own.

They lived by capturing trading vessels, and robbing them of their cargoes; and also, when they got hold of anyone who seemed to be a man of importance, they held him to ransom, making him pay a large sum of money before they would set him free.

They did this to Cæsar. Cæsar was a Roman of high rank. They told him that he must pay twenty talents for his ransom.

This was a large sum, as much as they thought they would be able to get from him. But Cæsar only laughed. He told them that he put a higher price on his liberty than that; he would pay them fifty talents. But

as he had not the money with him, he sent
some of his men to collect it from his friends
at home; and while he waited for the money
to come, he remained almost alone with the
pirates, having only two slaves to attend on
him.

The pirates were savage, blood-thirsty
men; often they killed people. Cæsar was
in their power, unarmed and helpless, but
he was not afraid of them. While he waited
for his ransom to be brought, he behaved
not like a prisoner, but as if he were their
lord and master. When he wanted to sleep
he would send word that they were not to
make a noise; and if they did, he scolded
them.

During the day, whatever sport or pastime
they were engaged in, he would go with them
and take part, often showing himself the
better man—more skilful and more active
than they in the games they played.

At other times he would sit down and write
poems and speeches; and when they were
finished he would make the pirates come
and hear them. And if there was anything
in what he had written that they did not
understand, he called them blockheads and

fools, and often warned them that one day he would hang all of them for their evil deeds.

The pirates took all this in good part, and thought him a very simple youth; for it seemed to them a great joke that one whom they held in their power, and could have killed any day, should behave as if he were their lord. And the joke seemed to them so good that they went on treating him more like a prince than a prisoner; and he went on treating them as though he had only to speak to be obeyed.

At last, after he had waited for it more than a month, his ransom was brought to him; and the pirates on receiving it let him go free, as they had promised.

They parted almost like friends; and when Cæsar told them that soon he was coming back to hang the whole lot of them, they took it for a joke.

But that is what Cæsar really did. Going back to the mainland, to the city of Miletus, from which his ransom had come, he got together ships and men. Then, returning to the island where he had been held prisoner, he fell upon the pirates unawares while their

HERE ARE THREE ROMAN SHIPS.
Notice the eye in the bow of the nearest ship, and the steersman
with his oar in the furthest ship.

ships were still riding at anchor in the
harbour. And having captured them all, he
carried them to the city of Pergamos, and
put them into jail. Then going to the
governor of the province, he told him what
he had done, and asked that they might be
put to death according to law.

But the governor was of a different mind.
He knew that somewhere the pirates had
much hidden wealth, and thinking to get
money out of them in exchange for their
lives, he told Cæsar that he would consider
the matter.

But Cæsar would not have it so. Taking
the matter into his own hands, he went back
to Pergamos; and there, from the jail where
he had put them, he drew out the pirates,

and as he had promised, when they thought
he did but jest, hanged every one of them.

In later days Cæsar became one of the
great conquerors of the world. He added
Gaul to the Roman Empire. And twice
with his Roman legions he landed in Britain,
though he did not stay there long. But this
great man, who commanded armies, and took
cities, and made captives of Kings, was once
a captive himself, as this story tells.

HEAD OF CÆSAR, FROM A BUST IN THE BRITISH MUSEUM.

ANNO DOMINI

JESUS, the Founder of the greatest religion of the world, was born in the land of Palestine nearly two thousand years ago, in the reign of Augustus, first Emperor of Rome. The beautiful Bible story tells us that He was born at Bethlehem, the city of David, and that shepherds and Wise Men received the news of His birth. But His home was in Nazareth, and for most of His life He worked as a carpenter, which was the trade of Joseph, His foster-father.

He was of Jewish race, and was brought up in the ancient Jewish religion.

Very little is known of Him till at the age of thirty He became a preacher and teacher of men. The common people heard Him gladly; all the things that He said filled them with joy and hope. He had a new message for the world, and He taught people in a new way. Most of the things He said when He began His public preaching were quite simple; the common folk could understand them; but, though simple, they had never been said before.

He taught men that God was the Father of all things, and that the Kingdom of Heaven was to be found in the hearts of men, and not in the great riches and powers of the world. He told the poor that it was more easy for them to come into this kingdom than for the rich; He told the simple that the way of truth was as open to them as to the wise.

On all these things He spoke as one who had been sent by God to declare them. He said that He was Himself the Son of God, and that by following Him men would have power to become sons of God also. It was this part of His teaching which roused the anger of the Jewish priests, and led them before long to make plans for His death.

The priests claimed that only they had the right to preach and teach religion; but Jesus went His own way, and taught men differently. For the carrying on of His teaching He chose twelve disciples, none of them learned; most of them were workmen like Himself; some were fishermen. It is very likely that only a few of them could read or write. But, made wise by His teaching, these men, after His death,

"THE FINDING OF THE SAVIOUR IN THE TEMPLE."

"And it came to pass, that after three days they found him in the temple, sitting in the midst of the doctors, both hearing them, and asking them questions. And all that heard him were astonished at his understanding and answers."—ST. LUKE ii. 46-47.

carried His message to other countries; and from their preaching, and the preaching of others who came after them, Christianity became the religion of Europe and of its people as they spread out into other parts of the globe.

At that time the Romans were the strongest people in the world; they held rule over most of Europe, and parts of Asia and Africa. Amongst other countries they ruled Palestine, the home of the Jews. The Jews had become a subject people; they paid tribute to Rome. But though they did so, they hated their rulers, and wished that they could find a leader who would help them to drive out the Romans and to become once more a free people. They were always looking for this to happen; and the man whom they looked for to be their leader they called the Messiah (which means anointed by God).

Now Jesus taught His followers that those who lived according to His teaching would be free, and that by so living they would bring about the Kingdom of God on earth. And because great multitudes came to listen to Him and followed Him as He went preaching from place to place, many thought that He must be this Messiah, and that the day would come when He would give the word and lead them to victory over the Romans.

But the kingdom which Jesus meant was not the kingdom of the Jews; nor did He wish to be the sort of Messiah they were expecting. He even spoke of His own death as being necessary for the coming of the Kingdom of God.

Yet more and more the belief grew among His followers that He was the one they had looked for. Even His disciples thought so, and disputed as to who should have first place when He had become their King. They could not get it out of their heads that He secretly meant to make Himself King of the Jews, and the Jewish race the greatest nation in the world.

Now while this was very much the wish and hope of the common people who were His followers, it was not at all to the liking of the priests and Rabbis, who were jealous of His great popularity with the multitude. The teaching of Jesus was not their teaching; and they saw quite well that, if His teaching was accepted by the people, their own power would be gone. So they began plotting among themselves how they could best get rid of Him.

Jesus had been preaching only for two years, but already He had the people with Him; and for that reason the priests did not dare to arrest Him openly on a charge of teaching the people falsely. It would be far safer, they thought, to have Him accused of planning to drive out the Romans and make Himself King; for then He would be tried in a Roman court, and put to death by Roman law.

They waited till the time of the great annual festival, the Jewish Passover, when Jesus and His disciples came up to Jerusalem to join in the feast. The people were expecting Him; they gave Him a great popular welcome. All day long crowds followed Him, and listened to His teaching. No doubt many were hoping that the day of their freedom was at hand.

While He was with the people His enemies made no sign. Then, late one night just before the Passover He was secretly arrested by order of the chief priests, and the same night was tried in the house of the High Priest, and condemned for blasphemy.

The next day He was brought before Pilate, the Roman Governor, and accused of forbidding the people to pay tribute to Cæsar, and of setting Himself up to be their King. And thus falsely charged with doing what so many of His own followers had wanted Him to do, He was condemned under the Roman law, and led out to be crucified.

The story of the death of Jesus upon the Cross is told in the four Gospels. It is the most wonderful story that has ever been written; and the death it tells of is the most wonderful death known to us since the world began. He was crucified by the Romans along with two thieves, that being the common form of death to which in those days criminals were condemned. By making Jesus die in this way, His enemies hoped to put an end not only to His life, but to His teaching also.

But this was not the end. The death on the Cross gave Christianity its crowning victory. Jesus had said that He would die, but He had also said that He would rise again to life. His own followers believed that He did so. On that belief the faith of the Christian religion is founded; and every year the great festival of Easter tells the world of the triumph that was won over death by Jesus, the Founder of Christianity.

Soon after this, His followers, led by the Apostles, began preaching the faith which Jesus had taught them, and which His death on the Cross had confirmed. From that day forward Christianity has been preached to the world; and there is no country or race which has not heard its message.

The birth of Jesus Christ dates the beginning of the age in which we are now living. When we write the letters A.D. they stand for Anno Domini, which means "in the year of our Lord." The date of the year, 1931, means that it is 1,931 years since He was born.

The ancient Romans dated their calendar from the year when the city of Rome was founded; but we date ours from the first Christmas Day, when, according to the reckoning of time which has come down to us, the child Jesus was born in Bethlehem.

THE KINGDOM

KINGS and crowns may come and may go;
  But here is a King that stays.
He came to the world; the world said " No "
  To the truth of His Kingly ways.

For the Kingdom of Heaven on earth, He
    taught,
  Was here in the heart of man.
And that was a Kingdom which few had sought
  Since first the world began.

And the Kingdom on Earth which man must
    seek,
  Ere a Kingly world can be,
Is to raise the fallen, and succour the weak,
  And let the slave go free.

With crown of thorns, and with wounded
    hands,
  Men made mock of a King
Whose word today through all the lands
  Of earth goes travailing.

With its wasting wars and its greed of gain,
  The world still says Him " No."
But the truth He taught will truth remain,
  Though Kings and crowns may go.

BRITAIN AND ROME: CÆSAR

B.C. 55

THE first great man we know of who came to Britain was Julius Cæsar. He was the greatest man of Roman history, and when he came to our island—nearly 2,000 years ago—the people of Britain were still savage and wild.

The Romans had great ships rowed by oars; they wore armour, they carried standards, they were very obedient to their generals, and they marched in rank as armies do today. Wherever they went they made roads to help their conquest of the country, and to open it for trade. In Britain we still have Roman roads, going from south to north and from east to west. The Romans were the strongest people in the world.

Julius Cæsar had already conquered Gaul, which we now call France. He had heard of an island lying on the other side of the Channel to the north, and he made up his mind to see it. Thus it was that, fifty-five years before the birth of Christ, Julius Cæsar came over to Britain.

He came with eighty ships and about 8,000 men, and, crossing by night, reached Dover in the early morning. But the Britons had heard of Cæsar's coming, and were there waiting for him. The high cliffs of Dover, defended by those fierce people, were too much for him; so he went along the coast looking for a more level landing-place. As he went, the Britons ran along the shore, keeping pace with his ships so as to prevent him from landing.

Towards evening he came to Deal, where the sea was shallow. Far out from the beach his great ships stuck in the sand. In order to land, his soldiers would have to jump overboard and wade. The Britons, on foot and in chariots, came charging down into the sea, throwing darts and javelins. The Romans hung back, fearing that from the deeper water, in their heavy armour, they would not be able to fight so well.

Night was beginning to fall; it seemed as if the army of proud Rome was about to be driven back by the wild people of our island.

THE LANDING OF THE ROMANS.

Then one man, a standard-bearer, did the brave thing which led the Roman legions to victory. The Roman standard of those days was a silver eagle carried on a pole; and the Romans would far rather die than let one of those eagles be taken by the enemy.

So this man, without waiting for the rest, sprang overboard, carrying the standard with him. " Jump, comrades !" he cried, " or will you see your eagle fall into the hands of the foe ?"

Then, to save their standard from being captured, the Roman soldiers followed him; and fighting their way through the water, they came to land, and the battle was won.

But that time the Romans did not stay long, or go far from the coast. Their ships were damaged in a great storm; some were wrecked, and others driven back southward across the Channel. So, after three weeks, Cæsar returned with his army to Gaul. But the next year he came again, and this time marched as far as the Thames, where he won a victory, and forced the Britons to make peace.

But the real Roman conquest of Britain was not made by Julius Cæsar. He returned to Gaul. Eight years later, he went back to Rome, and was there murdered by some of his own countrymen. But because Julius Cæsar was so great a man, all the Emperors --the rulers of Rome who came later—were called Cæsar.

The month of July—which means the month of Julius—is also named after him.

Now it was Julius Cæsar's nephew, Augustus, who became the first Roman Emperor; and it was in the reign of Augustus—as was told in the last story of Book II.—that Our Lord was born in a far distant corner of the Roman Empire.

Very soon after the Crucifixion of Our Lord, the Romans came once more to Britain. This time they conquered it, and it remained a part of the Roman Empire for nearly 400 years.

THE SANDS OF DEAL

OUT across the sands of Deal,
    Twenty centuries ago,
Ancient Britons, peal on peal,
    Heard loud trumpets blow;
And, across the blue waves leaping,
Ranged in rank, with long oars reaping,
Saw the Roman ships come sweeping
    Shoreward, row on row.

Out across the sands of Deal,
    Twenty centuries ago,
Britons matched 'gainst Roman steel
    Met with overthrow.
Out they went, with brawl and brattle,
Furious chariot-charge, and rattle
Of loud wheels all fanged for battle—
    Out, to face the foe.

Deep into the sands of Deal,
    Twenty centuries ago,
Conquering Cæsar drove his keel
    Where the tide lay low.

And as there his ships stayed stranded,
Lo ! the legions he commanded
Leapt into the waves, and landed,
    Driving back the foe.

There upon the sands of Deal,
    Twenty centuries ago,
Ruthlessly the Roman heel
    Trod the tribesmen low.
Then the sowing, now the reaping :
Gone is now all cause for weeping ;
Britain still, in Britons' keeping,
    Fears no foreign foe.

A BRAVE MONK AT THE ROMAN GAMES

A.D. 404

WHILE the Romans were conquering Britain, a great building called the Colosseum had been set up in Rome.

THE COLOSSEUM AS IT WAS.
Made largely of concrete; held 87,000 people

Here, on feast days and holidays, the Romans came and held their games. Some of their games were very cruel; trained bodies of men, called gladiators, fought and killed each other to amuse the onlookers. Regular battles would sometimes take place with 50,000 people looking on; and on a single day many scores of these fighters would be killed to amuse the people. On one occasion we read of tattooed Britons, who were prisoners of war, fighting in their chariots in the games at Rome.

There had always been some people in

A FIGHT IN THE COLOSSEUM.

The gladiator on the right has thrown his net over his opponent
to hamper him, and is striking at him with his trident,
which the other gladiator is parrying with his shield.

Rome who thought such games were wicked,
and tried to stop them. But because it was a
national custom, and because it was so excit-
ing to watch, the Romans kept these games
going on, even when most of the people in
Rome had become Christians.

Then one day a monk, named Telemachus,
who had come from Asia to Rome for this
sacred purpose, ran down into the arena
among all the fighters, and stood between
them, forbidding them to go on with such
a wicked game.

The people were furious at having their
game thus spoiled. They shouted, and shook

their fists, and threatened. And when Telemachus refused to go away, or let the game continue, a great number broke into the arena, and killed the brave monk by stoning him to death.

But it was the self-sacrifice of this monk from Asia which brought home to the Emperor the cruelty of these games. When the Emperor heard of the monk's death, he issued a law that the games should be stopped in Rome and in all the West. All over the Roman Empire, including Britain, these games had been popular. They began long before Christ was born, and it was one of the great blessings brought by the religion of Christ that the cruel games at last came to an end.

A GLADIATOR'S HELMET.

ST. PATRICK OF IRELAND

A.D. 389-461

THERE are no snakes in Ireland! The Irish have a legend that they were all driven down into the sea by St. Patrick, and there drowned!

St. Patrick is the patron Saint of Ireland, but he was not an Irishman. He was born in Britain at a time when the Romans were still ruling over the land, and he was given the Roman name of Patricius.

When he was a boy of sixteen, a band of Irish sea-robbers came and raided his father's farm; and along with many others they carried him away captive to Ireland. There he became the slave of an Irish chief, and for six years was his swineherd, looking after a drove of pigs in a mountain forest which was near by. It was there, as a slave, that he learned the Irish language.

Patrick had been a Christian from his birth. One day, while he was still a slave, he seemed to hear a voice which said: " Soon shalt thou return to thy native land." And

not long after, he heard it again, saying:
" Behold, now thy ship is ready !"

Believing this to be a voice from Heaven
sent for his guidance, he ran away from his
master; and making his way across Ireland,
he came to a seaport near Wicklow. There
he found a boat that was about to sail with
a ship-load of dogs; for at that time Irish
wolf-hounds were sold into other countries,
as the best breed of dog for the hunting of
wild beasts.

At first the master of the ship would not
let him come on board; and Patrick was
going away sorrowful and disappointed, when
he heard the sailors calling after him : " Come
quick; he wants you !"

So Patrick joined the crew and escaped
from slavery. But the ship did not take him
back to Britain. After a three days' voyage
they landed in France; and journeying
through the country they came to desert
places, where they could find neither food
nor shelter. They began to starve.

Then the shipmaster said to him : " You are
a Christian, and you say that your God is
so great He can do anything. Prove it to us
by praying that He will save our lives."

Patrick said: "It is quite true; with God nothing is impossible." And presently, as if in answer to his prayer, they met a drove of wild pigs, and with the help of their hounds, killed as many as they needed.

With their wolf-hounds for sale, they came at last to Italy; and there Patrick and his friends parted company. Drawn to a holy life, he stayed in that country, and learned Latin, and trained to become a priest.

But all the time he wanted to return to his own land of Britain; so, when the chance came, he went back from Italy to France, and for a time was at a monastery on an island, living the life of a monk. It was years before he got back to his own country; and when he did, it was only to leave it again. For one night he had a dream that a man came and handed to him a letter written in Irish; and the letter said: "Holy youth, come back to us, and walk among us as before." Then it seemed to Patrick that he heard also the voices of children calling, and asking him to come, so that they might be baptised and made Christians.

The call seemed to him so clear, that

AN EARLY MONASTIC CELL, ONE OF A GROUP OF FIVE THAT STILL EXIST IN IRELAND.

Notice the beehive-shaped roof and the small window with a cross of six white stones above it.

without delay he went back once more to the land where he had been a slave. He was now a priest; and soon he became a bishop.

At that time most of the people of Ireland and their Kings were still heathens; but as Patrick travelled from place to place, he was often kindly received, and given food and shelter; and wherever he stayed he made converts to the Christian faith.

While Patrick was making Christians of the natives, he also built churches. His first church was made out of an old wooden barn given to him by his first convert.

Wherever he went, men feared and respected him; and many stories are told of the power he had to punish wrong-doers. One man stole from him a yoke of oxen. Patrick said to him: " Thou hast done ill; thy land shall never profit thee." And a short time after, the sea broke in and covered all his fields, turning them into a salt marsh.

St. Patrick was greatly helped in his work of converting the people to Christ by the friendship of the High King of Ireland, though the King was not himself a Christian.

They were not friends at first. A story is told of how Patrick once celebrated the Feast of Easter by lighting fires on the side of a hill, on the very night when, under the old Druid religion, no fire must be lighted until the King had lighted one himself. But before the King had done so, he and his priests saw far away the fires of Patrick

shining through the night. Then the King
gathered his followers together, and set off
in nine chariots to take Patrick prisoner, and
punish him for what he had done. The
legend says that when summoned before the
King, Patrick was so fearless, and gave such
wonderful proofs of his faith in the power
of God to save him and his followers from
death, that the King let him go free without
punishment.

Not long afterwards, all the lesser Kings
of Ireland came together at the great
Feast of Tara,[1] to exchange counsel and
to pay homage to their High King. And
then it was agreed that the religion of Christ
should be allowed throughout the land, and
that protection should be given to it.

But though the High King thus made it
lawful for the Irish to become Christians, he
never became a Christian himself. When he
died he gave orders that no cross should be
put over his tomb; and he was buried, as all
his forefathers had been, standing upright,
and clad in full armour, like a warrior made
ready for battle.

[1] Twenty-one miles north-west of Dublin.

ST. BENEDICT, THE MONK, AND
ST. SCHOLASTICA, THE NUN

A.D. 480-543

BENEDICT was born in Italy, the son of rich and noble parents. But at the age of fifteen he felt called to a holy life of prayer and fasting; and leaving his father's house, he became a hermit, with a poor hut for shelter, meaning to live only on bread and water.

He left his home secretly, fearing that his parents would not let him go. But his old nurse, who loved him dearly, found out where he had hidden himself, and followed him; and for a while she lived with him, and looked after him, and cooked for him.

But after a time Benedict found that her care and good cooking made things too comfortable for him; and wishing to have nothing but what was necessary for life, he went away from her, and for three years lived all alone in a mountain cave, where another hermit brought food for him.

Now Benedict had beautiful manners; he was gentle and modest and kind; and everyone who met him loved him. People would

TWO MONKS PUZZLING OVER A DIFFICULT PASSAGE.

come to see him and to talk with him; and all who came went away happy, refreshed by the beauty of his character and the wisdom of his words.

Gradually his fame spread; and many hermits, living in those parts, came and begged him to be their head, and guide them in holy living.

Benedict would have liked better to be alone; but he granted their wish. Before long, however, the rule of life which he made for his followers seemed to some of them too hard to bear. So, wishing to get rid of him, one day they gave him a cup of wine which had poison in it. The legend tells us that, as he was making the sign of the cross over it before drinking, it fell out of his hand and all the wine was spilt. To the guilty ones this seemed a miracle; but when they confessed to Benedict the wicked plot they had made to kill him, he forgave them.

After this, Benedict went away again to a place where he could be alone; but it was not to be. So many hermits gathered round him, hoping to share his holy life, that he agreed to live with them and to make rules for their daily conduct. But it was not till some years later that he built the first home for monks—which we call a monastery.

This monastery was at a place called Monte Cassino, in Italy, on the very spot where once stood a temple to the Greek god Apollo. Here he founded the order of monks who are called Benedictines after his own name, and gave them the rule which has lasted to this day.

His fame went far and wide. One day the King of the Goths, hearing of his great holiness and wisdom, came to visit him. But wishing to find out how wise he was, the King disguised himself as a common soldier, and made his armour-bearer put on the royal robe. It was no use. Benedict knew the King at once. When the King found that here was a man who could read the secrets of hearts, he confessed to him many wrong things that he had done, and asked Benedict to teach him the way to a better life.

Benedict lived to see his order of monks increase greatly in number and in power. Many other monasteries were built and called after his name. It was a Benedictine monk, St. Augustine, who (as is told in a later story) preached the Gospel to the men of Kent; and later on, many of the greatest monasteries in England followed the Rule of St. Benedict.

Homes or convents for nuns were also built. The founder of the first of these was a sister of St. Benedict named Scholastica, who was led to the holy life by her brother's example.

These two loved each other dearly; but because they had taken to the religious life, living apart from the world, they could not often meet. But once every year Benedict would go to see his sister in her convent;

MASONS AT WORK IN THE ELEVENTH CENTURY, WHEN
MANY MONASTERIES WERE BUILT.
On the right they are bringing stones; and on the left they are
working a windlass (note the rope).

and this went on year by year until they had
both reached old age.

One year, when Benedict came to see her,
Scholastica felt it would be for the last time.
So, when the hour for his departure drew
near, she begged him to stay that night as
a guest of the convent. But this was against
the rule, which forbade a monk to pass the
night away from his own monastery; so
Benedict, in spite of his sister's earnest
entreaty, set out on his return. Hardly had

he started when a great storm came on and drove him back to the convent for shelter.

There he stayed that night, in prayer with the sister who had loved him so long and so dearly: and three days later she died.

Not long after Benedict himself felt sickness come on him, and knew that his end was at hand. He ordered his grave to be dug while he was still living; and six days later his monks buried him at the monastery of Monte Cassino, in a small chapel built over the very spot where once had stood the altar of the god Apollo.

And so the grave of St. Benedict is a symbol of the great change which had come over the world in those first centuries, when the religion of Christ was putting an end to the old pagan worship of Greece and Rome.

SCENES FROM CONVENT LIFE (THIRTEENTH CENTURY).

Two pilgrims received by nuns; then given something to drink; one is looked after when ill; then they are fed.

MOHAMMED, THE PROPHET OF THE DESERT

BORN A.D. 570

MOHAMMED was born at Mecca in Arabia. His father died the same year, and his mother died when he was only six. But he had an old grandfather, almost a hundred years old, who looked after him, and at his death, left him to the care of an uncle.

Mohammed was brought up in the old religion of Arabia. In those days the Arabs worshipped the sun and the stars, and other forms of nature. But a big black stone which was said to have been given by an angel to Abraham was one of the things that they held most sacred. Round the stone a temple had been built, called the Kaaba; and beside it was a holy well.

The well, and the stone, and the temple are still there; and thousands of pilgrims go every year to worship at Mecca, and to visit the birthplace of Mohammed, their great prophet. This big stone which they worshipped helped in the old days to keep the Arabs together and make them one people.

Except when they went trading on their camels, they did not often leave their own country, and so knew little of what other people were doing and thinking. One day the boy Mohammed went trading with his uncle; and it may have been in these early days that the boy came upon a group of people who had given up their old Arabian religion. They were not Christians, but they believed in one God; and before long Mohammed came to feel that this was a much better form of religion than that in which he had been brought up. He did not become Christian; but he did in time come to worship one God.

The next thing that we hear about Mohammed is that he became the steward of a rich widow, and before long they married and lived very happily together. After that nothing much happened until he was forty. Then one day, while he was praying in a cave where he had gone to be alone, Mohammed had his first vision of what seemed to him to be Divine Truth: the great law of life which showed him the true God.

THE GREAT MOSQUE AT MECCA, ROUND WHICH PILGRIMS WALK
SEVEN TIMES.

In the middle of the Mosque, and covered with a rich cloth
is the Kaaba, a rough stone building containing the black
stone, which every pilgrim kisses.

After that he had other visions, and out of these grew his religion, and also the great book which he wrote, called the Koran, which is the sacred book of his followers.

" There is one God, Allah : and Mohammed is His prophet," are the words in which all his followers declare their faith.

Mohammed set to work trying to make his people believe that there was only one God, and that all things were of His making, and could only live by His law. To us this does not sound strange; but it made many of his tribe very angry; and he had to hide in caves and desert places, and go in disguise, and at last to flee for his life.

When the city of his birth cast him out, he went, taking his followers with him, to another place which is now called Medina, the city of the prophet. Mohammed was then fifty-three. From that day of his flight to a strange city, his followers date the founding of their religion; for after that, they ceased to run and hide themselves; they faced all who came against them, and fought and beat them. And because of their success in war, many joined them, less for love of truth than for love of fighting.

So Mohammed's religion became a conquering religion, with brave fighters for its followers; and today nearly all the Mohammedan races are fighting races.

Many stories are told of Mohammed, but some of these, coming from people who hated him and his religion, are not true.

One of the stories told against him was that, before letting his followers come to see him, he would secretly put grains of corn into the hollow of his ear; and then he would put a pigeon upon his shoulder; and when the pigeon began pecking the corn out of his ear, he would pretend that it was an angel whispering messages from God.

It is an amusing story; but there is no proof that it is true. There is another story which shows that he was an honest man who would not pretend what was false. People had begun asking him for miracles to prove the truth of his teaching. Mohammed said: " I can work no miracles. I can only preach truth." And he told people that the greatest of all miracles was life, in which the ways of God were to be seen and learned.

To the end of his days, even when his followers thought him the greatest man who had ever been born, Mohammed lived quite simply. He ate barley-bread, and drank nothing but water. He patched his own cloak, and mended his own shoes. And though he was a fighter, he still believed that peace was the best thing in the world. This was the meaning of the new form of greeting which he taught to his disciples: " Salaam," meaning " Peace (be upon you)." The word has come down to this day, and is used by his followers.

Mohammed lived about the same time as St. Augustine, the monk who brought the Christian Faith to the people of Kent. Today there are living over 200 millions of his followers. Many millions of these live in the British Empire.

A FOURTEENTH-CENTURY ARAB PICTURE OF MOHAMMED ON HORSEBACK, WITH ANGEL GABRIEL ON HIS NEAR LEFT.

THE FLIGHT THROUGH THE DESERT

RIDE ! Ride !
    And God be our Guide !
Safe ways are narrow,
And dark ways are wide.
    Death runs behind us,
    Foes seek to find us,
    Night stands to blind us:
God be our Guide.

    Ride ! Ride !
    Keep close at my side,
    O ye that have followed,
    Whose faith has not died.
There in the city came friends to betray us;
Outside the city were foes to waylay us;
The hands of our haters were ready to slay us !
    Ride ! Ride !
    And God be our Guide.

They are the many, and we are the few;
We are the weak, and they are the strong;
But a work has been put in our hands to do,
And to us, not to them, shall the Kingdom
        belong.

Ride ! Ride !
God is our Guide !
They shall fall from their pride
To the truth they denied.

For they are the blind
    Whose gods are many;
Soon shall they find
    They have not any.
Even or odd,
    They shall number as none:
There is no God
    In this world but One.

Ride ! Ride !
God is our Guide !
Safe ways are narrow,
And dark ways are wide.
    Death runs behind us,
    Foes seek to find us,
    Night stands to blind us,
God is our Guide.

STORIES OF EARLY ENGLAND

(a) St. Augustine, A.D. 597

THE story of St. Patrick shows that there were Christians in Britain in Roman times. When the Romans left, the Angles and Saxons invaded our land and made it their own, and called it England. For a time the Christian Church died out in some parts of our island. Then the Christian religion was again preached by monks who came from Rome.

One day a Roman priest named Gregory, who afterwards became Pope Gregory the Great, was walking in the market-place of Rome. There he saw, waiting to be sold as slaves, some beautiful boys with fair hair; and because they were so unlike those of his own dark race, he stopped to ask what country they came from. From the island of Britain, he was told, of a race called Angles.

Now in the Latin language the words Angel and Angle are almost the same. So Gregory, speaking in Latin, said: " Well are they named; for they have angel faces."

But when he heard that they were heathen

and came from a heathen land, he felt sorry for them; and it became his great wish to go and convert England to the faith of Christ.

This, however, he was not able to do, having then to obey others. But when he became Pope he remembered his past wish.

So he chose a certain Benedictine[1] monk, named Augustine, who was a good preacher, and sent him to England with a band of forty monks.

Having landed in Kent, they came to Canterbury, singing as they journeyed, and carrying crosses and banners; and all the people of the country flocked to meet them. The King of Kent, whose name was Ethelbert, and whose Queen was a baptised Christian, received them kindly, and gave them leave to preach their Gospel to all. Not long afterwards he himself was converted, and so became the first Christian King in England.

Later, from Canterbury, monks went out north and west, to try to convert other kingdoms of Britain to the Christian Faith. One of these monks, as the next story tells us, went to Northumbria.

[1] See Story IV.

(b) How Good King Edwin became a Christian

A.D. 627

In the kingdom of Deira (see map), there was a King who died when his son Edwin was yet a child. The land had no head who could rule; and Ethelfrith, King of Bernicia (see map), came in and took possession.

Those who were faithful to their old lord brought the child Edwin for safety to the care of Redwald, King of East Anglia; and in Redwald's court Edwin grew up in exile, a King robbed of his kingdom; and Redwald was kind to him, and promised to be his friend.

But Ethelfrith, the usurper, did not wish that Edwin should have anyone to befriend him; so he sent word to Redwald, promising him rich gifts if he would have Edwin slain. When Redwald refused, Ethelfrith sent again, promising him more.

When Redwald had refused a second time to betray his friend, Ethelfrith made him a still larger offer, and said: " Slay, or deliver him into my hands, and all this shall be yours.

If you will not do as I ask, I will come and make war against you, and take him myself."

This threat made Redwald afraid, for the Northumbrians were stronger than the East Angles, and Ethelfrith was a man well-skilled in war. So he said to the messengers: "Tarry here awhile, and either I will slay Edwin, or will deliver him into your hands."

But Edwin had a friend who, having got word of it, came and told him of his danger, and begged him to flee for his life. Edwin said: "Redwald is my friend; he and I have sworn to be true to each other in word and deed. If he wishes to slay me, let him! Seeking the help of strangers, I should only fare worse. I will stay where I am."

After his friend had left him, Edwin sat alone, very sad at heart, not knowing what would happen to him. While he so sat, a stranger came and stood by him, and asked him of his trouble. Edwin trusted the stranger, and told him all his grief. The stranger said: "What will you give to the man who shall free you from your fear, and turn the heart of Redwald to be your friend again?"

Edwin replied: " I will give him all that is now mine."

The stranger said again: " And if he promises that you shall see the defeat of your enemy, and be King once more in your own land—what will you give to him then?"

Edwin replied: " I will give him as much as he likes to ask of me."

" And if," said the stranger, " when you have gained your victory and are on your throne again, this man comes and tells you of a new life and a better law than you have yet known, will you then believe and do as he tells ?"

Edwin replied: " If all these things come to pass, I will obey the word of so wise a man, whatever he tells me."

Then said the stranger: " So shall it be." And laying his hands on Edwin's head, he said: " Take this for a sign; and remember, when it comes, to do as you have promised."

So saying, the stranger departed. And, not long after, all happened as the stranger said it should happen. For Redwald repented of his evil thought, and sending away the messenger of Ethelfrith, prepared to do battle for the life of his friend. And

when Ethelfrith was on his way to invade
East Anglia, Redwald came upon him by surprise, on the banks of the river Idle, which is
in the county of Nottingham; and Ethelfrith's
army was defeated, and he himself was slain.

So Edwin returned in triumph to his
own land, and became lord of all Northumbria. And he ruled peacefully and well,
and was loved by all his people.

Now up till this time Edwin had been a
heathen, worshipping Woden like the rest of
his people. But wishing to marry, he chose
a princess named Ethelburga, who was sister
to the King of Kent; and she and her brother
were Christians. For which reason she at
first refused him; but having a great love for
her, he promised that she should be free in her
own religion, and that all who came with her
should be free to serve God in their own way.

So Ethelburga became his wife, and brought
with her a Christian priest named Paulinus;
but Edwin and his followers remained
heathen. None the less he was a good ruler,
and his people loved him. And to strengthen
his realm, he fought and overcame all who
came against it; and having won many
victories returned in peace to his own

house, where on Easter Day his wife had given birth to a son.

For love of her he allowed his son to be baptised, but was not baptised himself; for he had not yet made up his mind to be a Christian.

But one day, as he sat deeply thinking, and wondering which was the true God—his own god Woden, or the God of the Christians —the priest Paulinus came and laid his hands on his head and said: " My son, knowest thou this sign ?"

Edwin remembered, and fell at his feet trembling, and said: " Tell me what I must do."

Paulinus said: " Become a Christian, for that is the new life and the new law of which long ago I spoke to thee."

Then Edwin believed the word of Paulinus and became a Christian, because everything which Paulinus, as a stranger, had promised him had now come true. But indeed Edwin had long since been a Christian at heart, and had done good things. It is told of him that throughout his realm, at every spring of water by the wayside, he put up stakes and hung brazen cups on them, so that men might drink. And for love of him the cups were not stolen.

In the city of York, which was the capital of his kingdom, Edwin built a church of stone on the spot where the great minster now stands: and he named it after the Apostle St. Peter, as the minster is still named to this day. Some years later, Edwin was defeated and slain in battle by the two Kings of Mercia and Wales, who had joined together against him; and his head was brought to York and buried in the porch of the church which he had begun.

(c) BEDE, THE FATHER OF ENGLISH HISTORY

A.D. 673-735

BEDE WRITING.
(Notice pen and knife)

In Early England the Church was the home of learning; for the monasteries gave to scholars the peace and safety they could not find in the outside world.

So it was a most happy chance that Bede—the Father of English History

—was taken into a monastery while still a child. It is from Bede's history of Britain we get the two stories we have just read.

Now Bede was only seven years of age when the Abbot of Jarrow took charge of him. Jarrow was a large monastery in the north of England, which followed the Rule of St. Benedict; and by good fortune the Abbot had brought a large store of books from Rome to his own monastery.

For more than fifty years Bede lived in Jarrow monastery, studying, and writing, and teaching. "All my life," he said, "I spent in that same monastery, giving my whole attention to the study of the Holy Scriptures, and between the hours of regular discipline and the duties of singing in the church, I always took pleasure in learning, or teaching, or writing something."

As a writer and a teacher Bede became famous even in his own day. In the course of his life he wrote more than forty books, on many subjects such as the stars, arithmetic, medicine, grammar, poetry, music, religion, and history.

There, in his quiet monastery, he gathered together all the facts he could find for the first history of England that had ever been written.

He was also a great teacher. As many as 600 monks, besides others who came from a distance, sat at his feet and listened to his wisdom. Because he taught in it, Jarrow became the greatest school of learning in the whole country. His fame went far. The Pope sent asking him to go to Rome; but Bede remained in his own land, always hard at work, never idle.

After living for sixty-two years he died. The story is told how, even when he was dying, he still went on with his work. Too weak to write himself, he dictated the words to a youth who sat at his side. When he was not dictating, he talked to his pupils, and sang psalms with them.

His last piece of work was the translation of the early chapters of St. John's Gospel. A day came when the youth, seeing how weak and ill he was, said to him: "Most dear master, there is only one more chapter to be done; but I think that now it is too hard for thee." "No," said Bede, "it is easy. Take thy pen and write quickly."

The work went on; it was almost finished.

Bede rested for a while, and used the time to divide among his friends and scholars the few things which he possessed—spices, napkins, and incense are some of the gifts mentioned.

Then the youth said to him: " There is still one more sentence which waits to be written." Bede gave him the translation: the youth wrote it down.

" Now that is done," said the youth. " Aye, done !" replied his master. " Thou speakest truth. Help me to sit in yonder place where I have been wont to pray."

The youth did so. Bede sat down on the pavement of his cell, and, with failing breath, sang the " Gloria " for the last time.

So ended the life and work of the first writer of English history, who, ever since that day, has been known as the Venerable Bede.

(d) ALFRED THE GREAT
871-901

Of all the Kings of Early England, King Alfred was the best and the greatest. To no other of our Kings has the title of " Great " been given; and though he stands so

far back in history, we still think of him as one
of the great makers of England.   Why is this?

The answer is that he was great no less in
peace than in war, and it was he who saved
England for the English from heathen in-
vaders whom we call the Danes.

In the year 870, Edmund, King of East
Anglia, had been killed by the Danes,[1] and
their armed bands had brought half the
country to rack and ruin.   At Peterborough,
an old record tells us, " they burned and broke,
slew abbots and monks, and so dealt with
what they found there that they brought it
to nothing."   It seemed then as if the whole
of England would soon be conquered by the
heathen Danes.

But in the following year, when Alfred
became King of the West Saxons, so many
battles were fought against the Danes that
871 was called the " year of battles."   Sometimes Alfred won, sometimes he lost.   But
the Danes were so wearied and weakened by
these battles that at last they made peace;
and for four years there was no more war
between them and the West Saxons.

Then came war again, and for Alfred and

[1] See the story of St. Edmund in Book I.

his people things went so ill, that he was forced with only a few followers to go and hide himself among the woods and marshes of Athelney in Somerset. Little hope seemed left, for the Danes had almost completely conquered the land.

But Alfred never despaired. Very quietly and secretly, from his hiding-place, he began to gather a new army. His people loved him; they hungered to have their King back again; and when at last he came out of hiding all the men of Wessex came to join him; and after a quick march of two days he came upon the Danes at Ethandune,[1] and there utterly defeated them. His victory was so great that he was able to make his own terms of peace; and one of these was that Guthrum, the King of the Danes, should become a Christian.

Alfred returned to Athelney; and there presently came Guthrum, with thirty of his chief warriors, to be baptised, and King Alfred stood as his godfather. Then for twelve nights Alfred feasted Guthrum, and sent him away loaded with gifts.

King Alfred, having now made peace for his kingdom, began to make wise laws, and

[1] Edington, near Westbury, in Wiltshire.

to restore peaceful customs and to revive learning. Even the school of learning, so peacefully founded by Bede[1] in the north of England, had been broken up by the long horrors and waste of war; and the people had fallen back into ignorance.

King Alfred, himself a scholar, led the way. He began translating books from Latin into the English of his day, which, though very unlike English as we speak it now, was then the language of the common people.

To help him in his work Alfred gathered about him teachers and scholars from other countries. One of these was a Welshman named Asser, who afterwards wrote King Alfred's Life. Another, John the Old Saxon, came from the region of the Elbe, and his ancestors probably belonged to the fierce heathen tribes of Germany who had fought against Charlemagne,[2] that other great King of early Christian Europe.

Alfred himself tells us in one of his books that " before all this ravaging and burning by the Danes, when the churches were filled with books and sacred vessels, God's servants abounded, yet they knew very little of the

[1] See Story VI. (c).   [2] See next story.

contents of their books, because they were not written in their own language." " Formerly men came from beyond our borders, seeking wisdom in our own land," as Charlemagne had sent for Alcuin of York to teach his people; " now, if we are to have wisdom at all, we must look for it abroad. So great was the decay of learning among Englishmen that there were very few on this side of the Humber, and I ween not many north of it, who could understand the Mass, or translate a letter from Latin into English. No, I cannot remember one such, south of the Thames, when I came to the throne."

This good and wise King, who thus cared for learning and sought always to give peace to his people instead of war, was also blessed with a happy home and a good wife. They had five children, all of whom proved worthy of their father. Of one, named Edward, we read that when he was not hunting or engaged in other manly exercise, he spent his time, in company with his sister, in " learning the psalter or books of Saxon poetry, showing gentleness towards all, both natives and foreigners."

This boy became King, as Edward the

Elder, on his father's death; and he proved himself one of the best of English Kings.

But of no English King is so much good told, and so little evil, as of King Alfred the Great. We still have, in the great Museum at Oxford, something which actually belonged to him, and which he must often have worn. It was found at Athelney. It is a jewel set in a band of metal; and round it are engraved the old Saxon words, "Aelfred mec heht gewyrcan," which in modern English mean, "Alfred ordered me to be made."

KING ALFRED'S JEWEL.

THE EMPEROR WHO COULD
NOT WRITE

A.D. 800

ONE of the greatest kings in history was called Charlemagne, which means Charles the Great. He was nearly seven feet high, and very strong. He became the ruler of the lands which are now France, Germany, and Italy; yet he could not read or write.

There was nothing strange about that, for eleven hundred years ago very few people could do either. What is much more strange is that when such a great and wise man began trying to learn he could not do so. He tried to teach himself, and his wife tried to teach him; but he had begun too late.

What most of us find easy, the great Charlemagne found impossible. He used to go to bed every night with his writing tablets under his pillow; and he would wake up in the night and start trying to do his letters. Yet it was no good; writing would not come to him.

But, because he loved learning, he encouraged schools; and he invited to his palace the learned Alcuin of York, who had himself been taught by one of Bede's pupils. And though Charlemagne could not write himself, he asked Alcuin to invent a better style of writing. In those days, and for hundreds of years later, all books were written by hand; and the early books were very difficult to read, the writing not being plain. So Alcuin, by the Emperor's orders, made a better handwriting, in a style which was followed in the beautiful books of the Middle Ages down to the time when books began to be printed.

Explicit Liber Secundus.
Incipit Liber Tertius
Sanctissima Mariae paenitentis historia quae...

WRITING IN CHARLEMAGNE'S TIME.

Into the schools which he started, the great Emperor would go himself and question the boys in class, to find out if they understood what they were being taught; and those who were idle he scolded. The story goes that one day he went into a church, where children had come to be baptised; and there he started to question them about the Christian religion. Finding that they did not understand it, he sent them away, and told them not to come back to be baptised till they knew better.

Also, in the royal chapel, the clerks who read the lessons had each to be ready every time, in case he should be chosen as reader; for the Emperor would point with his staff to one of them, and at once he had to start reading, and read on without making a single mistake, until the Emperor gave a cough, which was the sign that the reading should stop.

It is not often that we hear of a

CHARLEMAGNE ON HORSEBACK.

King putting so high a value on something he could not do himself; but Charlemagne, though he was the greatest man of his day, and the highest in rank, used to tell his people that high birth alone was worth nothing, and that the only way to his favour was through learning and industry.

WILLIAM THE CONQUEROR

1066-1087

I N the year 1066, a great comet appeared in the heavens, and shone for seven days with a great light. Because it had a long tail, men in those days called it a " hairy star." All believed that it foretold some great event.

COMET FROM THE BAYEUX TAPESTRY.

So when William the Conqueror and his army landed in England, and won the battle of Hastings, many thought that the star had been sent to foretell his coming.

William was Duke of Normandy. On September 27th, 1066, he crossed the English Channel with his army, and landed at Pevensey Bay in Sussex.

A story of that famous landing tells how the Norman ships, ranged side by side in a long line, cast anchor all together; and at once men, horses, and weapons were sent ashore. As soon as the anchors had been cast, the ships were made fast to land; then out over the sides climbed sailors and soldiers, each at his appointed task. Out in turn came men carrying shields and saddles in great loads; then came the war-horses and the baggage-horses, the archers with their bows and their quivers full of arrows. Next came the knights, fully armed, with shields slung at their necks and helmets laced; and down the front of each helmet ran a long nose-piece to protect the face of the man who wore it. After them came the carpenters and woodcutters, each carrying a great axe, and with the tools of their trade slung at their sides.

So in quick time the whole army was landed, fit and ready to march inland to the place of battle. A few miles from Hastings, William met and defeated Harold, the last of the Saxon Kings; and from that victory followed the Norman conquest of England.

The story is told that when William himself landed on our coast he tripped and fell. And because he knew that those who saw him fall would think it a bad omen, as he lay he took up two handfuls of soil and cried: "Thus I take possession of this land!" And so, turning his accident into an omen of victory, he rose and went on his conquering way.

In the twenty years that followed, while he tamed England to rule by foreigners, he proved himself a great but a stern ruler of men.

In later life he had another fall which did not turn out so fortunately. Back in Normandy, fighting to put down revolt, he took and set fire to a town; and as he rode into the still burning ruins, his horse trod on a hot cinder and threw him heavily against the saddle, from which injury he died.

NORMANS ARRIVING AT PEVENSEY.
Notice ships, men and their shields, and horses' heads. (*From Bayeux Tapestry.*)

WILLIAM THE CONQUEROR THROWN FROM THE SADDLE
AT THE SIEGE OF ROUEN.

HEREWARD THE WAKE

THOUGH the English were defeated at the battle of Hastings, in some parts of the country they still fought for many years against the foreigner; and in East Anglia they had a brave leader named Hereward the Wake—which means " the Watchful."

Hereward had only a few followers. The Normans were much the stronger, and hunted him from place to place. But they could not catch him; for though he had not many men, he had many strong places of his own where the Normans could not follow him.

In those days England had in it many islands; the islands are not islands any longer, but some of their names remain. One of these was and is still called the Isle of Ely. All round Ely in those days were fens and undrained marshes, and the land lay mostly under water; and where the water left off were beds of mud, overgrown by reeds.

Among those beds of reeds, which spread for miles and miles, Hereward and his followers hid themselves. Whenever they saw their chance to take the Normans by surprise, they came out and fought; and when the number of the Normans became too much for them, they disappeared again into the reed-beds.

Thus, for many years Hereward and his men kept on fighting bravely; but they were beaten at last. Some writers tell us that Hereward himself was killed fighting; others say that, when the fight became hopeless, he accepted William the Conqueror as his lord, and died in peace.

After his death, the English, who loved his memory, told many stories about him and his brave followers: of how often they fought, a few against many, and time after time escaped from what seemed certain death.

One day Hereward, wishing to find out at what time and in what way the enemy was going to attack him, disguised himself as a pedlar. He loaded his horse with pots and pans, and led it into the Norman camp. There he started to sell his wares, and all the while, keeping his eyes and ears open, he learned the news he had come for.

Suddenly, Hereward saw, by the look on

HEREWARD HIDDEN UNDER THE PILE OF REEDS.

a man's face, that under his disguise he was
discovered. Hereward did not give the man
time to speak; jumping on his horse, he
threw all his pots and pans at the heads of
those who were nearest him, and setting his
horse at a hard gallop, he rode them down.
Before any had time to stop him, he was out
of the camp, with all the Norman horsemen
galloping after him. But the shouting of a

hundred men could not make their horses as quick as Hereward's horse, which he called " Swallow." So, helped by " Swallow," Hereward got safely back to his own people and told them his news.

Another time, he and his small band of followers, finding themselves surrounded, went and lay down in one of the flat-bottomed boats used by the reed-cutters. Then over them was laid a great pile of reeds, which must have almost smothered them; and in front of the pile stood a boatman with his long punting-pole, pushing the boat slowly on its way down the reedy channels and out into the open river beyond. And the Normans, who stood guarding the banks, let the boat go through, thinking that it held nothing but a pile of reeds.

Hereward was a brave man; and his courage has made him famous ever since. But that boatman, whose name is forgotten, must have been a brave man too, playing his part so well, while knowing all the time how on him depended the life not only of Hereward and the rest, but his own. For had the Normans found out what he was doing, they would have killed him without mercy.

THE ARROW IN THE NEW FOREST

A.D. 1100

ONE of the most beautiful parts of England is the New Forest. But though it still bears that name, the Forest is a very old one. More than 800 years ago a King made it his hunting-ground. In order to do so, he destroyed all the huts and villages which lay within its borders, and removed the peasants who lived in them, so that he might go hunting everywhere, and that the game might not be disturbed.

The King who did this was William the Conqueror. His son, the next King, was William Rufus, so called because of his red hair. He was not a good King. People hated him.

One day he went hunting in the Forest with one of his courtiers named Walter Tyrell. Before nightfall the King was found lying dead under a tree, killed by an arrow.

Tyrell, afraid of being charged with having murdered the King, did not wait to tell the story; he rode away and escaped out of the country to France. What really happened was never quite known. It is generally believed that an arrow from Tyrell's bow struck a branch of the tree under which the King was riding, and turning aside, pierced his breast and killed him.

A poor charcoal-burner named Richard Purkiss found the King's body, and putting it upon his cart brought it to the nearest village. From there it was carried for burial to Winchester, the cathedral at which in those days the English Kings used to be crowned.

But because Rufus was a bad man and a bad King, the priests would " say no mass for him and toll no bell." And when, seven years later, the tower under which his body lay fell down, it was taken as a sign that one so wicked was unfit for Christian burial.

Today, in the Forest, on the spot where the King's body was found, stands a stone called the Rufus Stone; and there are still living in the New Forest descendants of the man in whose cart the body was brought back for burial.

THE WHITE SHIP

A.D. 1120

AFTER a bad King came a good one.
Henry I, the third of the Norman
Kings, was a great man like his father,
William the Conqueror. He governed
sternly but justly, and cared well for the
country over which he ruled.

Though foreign-born, Henry married an
English wife called Matilda. She was de-
scended on her mother's side from the old
Saxon Kings, and her father was King of
Scotland.

Henry I was not only a good ruler, he was
a scholar also. He knew several languages,
and could read and write, which in those
days Kings could seldom do. To his father,
the Conqueror, who was himself nothing of
a scholar, he once said: " A King who
cannot read is a crowned ass."

In the latter part of Henry's reign came
a great sorrow. He had an only son, Prince
William; and father and son had gone over
to Normandy together to put an end to the
disorders which were bringing that country

to ruin. On their return to England they came by different boats. Later than the rest, Prince William and his men put to sea in a boat called *The White Ship*.

The crew, proud of the honour of having on board the King's son and heir, asked that they might have wine to drink his health. The Prince ordered a barrel of wine to be brought on board, and the crew drank too much.

It was already getting dark as they set out on their voyage. Before they had gone far, the tipsy pilot steered the ship against a rock which hardly showed above the water. The ship, badly holed, began to sink. A boat was lowered, and the Prince was already safely in and clear of the wreck, when he heard the cries of his sister, who, in the darkness and confusion, had been left on board. He ordered the boatmen to return; and as they came again under the ship's side, those who had remained on the sinking vessel leapt down into the boat to save themselves, and under their weight the boat sank and all were drowned.

The only man left to tell the tale was a butcher of Rouen, named Berold, who clung to a floating spar all night and was picked up by some fishermen next day. Through him word came over to England that the King's son was dead. At first nobody dared tell Henry the news; but at last they sent to him a little page, who fell bitterly weeping at the King's feet, and told him that his son had been drowned.

When Henry heard that news he fell senseless to the ground; and it was said that after that day he was never again seen to smile.

THE WRECK OF THE WHITE SHIP.

THE KING'S JESTER AND
THE HOSPITAL

A.D. 1100

KING HENRY I had many gay courtiers, but Rahere was the merriest of
them all. " He was," says the chronicler,
" a pleasant-witted gentleman." By his
jokes and flattery he made friends with
everyone, and in pageants and gay feasts
provided amusement for the Court. Wherever he went, laughter followed him.

But this life of pleasure did not long satisfy
Rahere. A time came when, in the words
of the chronicler, " God converted this man
from the error of youth, and added to him
many gifts of virtue; for they are often
lowly born whom our Lord chooses to
confound the mighty."

It may well be that Rahere's change of
heart was helped by an event which about
that time brought grief to the whole nation.
The terrible news of the drowning of the
King's son, Prince William, and his young
sister, plunged the King and his whole court
into mourning.

BOY HAVING HIS TONGUE
EXAMINED.

BOY NOT FEELING WELL.

At all events, not long after, Rahere quitted
the court, became a monk, and left England
on a pilgrimage to Rome. On the way he
met with many perils, for at that time
travelling in Europe was dangerous. The
roads were haunted by fierce brigands, and
hungry packs of wolves roamed through the
countryside.

Escaping from these dangers, Rahere,
when he got to Rome, fell a victim to the
plague which was then raging, and nearly
died of it. During his sickness he made a
vow that, if his life were spared, he would
go back to London and there build a hospital
for the sick poor.

As soon as he was strong enough, he started

to return home. On his way he had a dream, and that dream was the cause why the great Hospital, which he founded, stands where it does in London today, and why it is called St. Bartholomew's.

For during his stay in Rome, Rahere often went to pray in a church dedicated to St. Bartholomew. In his dream the Saint seemed to appear to him in a shining light; and he heard a voice saying, " Go and build a house in my name at Smithfield, and I will be its master and patron, and watch over it."

Rahere, awaking from his dream, renewed his vow, and continuing his journey in haste, arrived in London; and from London, which then stood within walls, he went out into the open country of Smithfield beyond.

Now at that time Smithfield was all muddy swamp and marsh, and did not look like a fit place for building a hospital. But the land belonged to the King, and Rahere, because of his dream, went to the King and begged that it might be given him.

The King, touched by his zeal and devotion, granted his request; and for ten years with the citizens of London to help him,

Two Doctors by a Patient's Bedside.
(*From a Fifteenth-Century Manuscript.*)

Rahere worked at draining the marsh, laying foundations, and building walls. And now, on the very spot, where he and his fellow-citizens laboured eight hundred years ago, stands the great Hospital which is called

" Bart's." It is very much bigger, and covers much more ground now, than the Hospital built by Rahere. But there in Smithfield was built London's first Hospital—the first, indeed, that had ever been built in England.

When the Hospital was finished, King Henry I gave to it a charter of right over the land around it, so that it might remain a freehold for ever; and the words of that old charter are still to be read:

" Let it have," said the King, " all liberties " (or privileges) " and free customs in all things which belong to the same, in wood and in plain, in meadows and pastures, in waters and mills, in ways and in paths, in pools and vineyards, in marshes and fisheries, in granges and copses, within and without, and in all places now and for ever. And I will maintain and defend this place even as my crown. And let this place be perpetually defended by the protection of Kings."

Kings have defended it in the past; but now its best defence is the love people have for it, because of the great good it has done in the world, healing the sick and saving thousands from suffering.

A FAMOUS ARCHBISHOP AND
A FAMOUS CATHEDRAL

A.D. 1170

OF all the cathedrals in England, Canterbury is the most famous—and this for many reasons. It was to Canterbury, as already told, that St. Augustine came from Rome to preach to the men of Kent. In due course Augustine became the first Archbishop of Canterbury.

In the Cathedral now stands what is called the Chair of St. Augustine; it is made of stone, and in that chair, for hundreds of years, each new Archbishop has been enthroned.

From St. Augustine's day to our own, there have been ninety-seven Archbishops of Canterbury. One, the best known of all, was Thomas Becket; and because of what happened to him the fame and wealth of the Cathedral increased greatly.

Thomas Becket was the friend and courtier of King Henry II, the grandson of Henry I, and the two friends used to have games together. Wherever the King went, riding, hunting, or on journeys of state, Becket went with him. Henry made him his chancellor, or chief secretary, and Becket served him faithfully and well; everything that he did pleased the King. So when a new Archbishop had to be appointed, it was the King's wish that Becket should be chosen.

But no sooner was Becket made Archbishop, than he ceased to serve the King as he had done formerly.

There was a great quarrel about the rights of the King and the rights of the Church; the King and the Archbishop were both men of strong will and obstinate. The quarrel got so fierce that Becket at last fled the country, and for six years there was no Archbishop at Canterbury. Then the King allowed Becket to return. But no sooner was Becket back in England than they started quarrelling again.

Complaints of what Becket was doing came over the sea to Normandy, where the King was then staying. In a rage, the King cried: " Will nobody rid me of this quarrelsome priest ?"

Four Norman knights heard what the King said. Without a word to anyone, they

THE MURDER OF BECKET.—A picture made some twenty years afterwards. Notice the four knights on the left. FitzUrse, who has a shield with a bear on it, is striking the first blow; this, however, only dashed off the cap of Becket, which you can see falling to the ground. Grim, Becket's most faithful follower, is on the right holding the cross-staff.

mounted their horses and made their way to the coast.

They crossed the Channel and rode fast to Canterbury. Within the doors of the Cathedral they met the Archbishop. They called him a traitor, and threatened to kill him if he would not yield himself a prisoner into their hands.

But Becket was fearless. "If all the swords in England were now at my head, I would not yield," he replied to them. At that they fell upon him; and in the struggle Becket was slain.

News of this dreadful deed went through all Europe; everyone heard of it with horror. The murder of an Archbishop within the walls of his own Cathedral frightened people. They feared that the curse of God would fall upon a land where such a thing had been done.

Because of his rash words, the King himself was held by many to be guilty of the Archbishop's death. The King said he was innocent; but because his word had been taken to cover the deed, he went to Becket's tomb, and there, as an act of penance, allowed himself to be publicly scourged by the monks.

Becket had died defending the claims of the Church against the claims of the King; and the people believed him to be a true martyr. Thomas the Archbishop became Thomas the Saint; and because of Becket's martyrdom, Canterbury became the richest as well as the most famous of English cathedrals, and Becket himself the most famous of English saints. For more than three hundred years after his death, pilgrims came from abroad, and from all over England, to worship at his shrine.

One of the first great poems in the English language was called the " Canterbury Pilgrims," as is told later in this book. It was written by Chaucer two hundred years after Becket's death, in the reign of King Edward III. It tells how a band of pilgrims went from London to Canterbury, keeping each other company, and telling stories by the way: a squire and a knight, a monk, a nun, and a friar, a parson and his brother the ploughman, various men of business, all going together on a holiday, with Canterbury as their goal.

Four hundred years after Becket's death, when another Henry (the VIIIth) broke up the monasteries and robbed them of their treasures, all the jewels and rich gifts which had been laid upon the shrine of St. Thomas were carried away from the Cathedral. No one knows now what became of them.

And what became of the body of Becket? Even of that we are not sure. But some years ago, when work was going on in the undercroft of the Cathedral, under the floor was found, in a stone coffin, the skeleton of a very tall man over six feet in height; and on the broken skull was the mark of a blow. This may have been the body of Thomas Becket, whose death brought to the Cathedral such riches and so much fame.

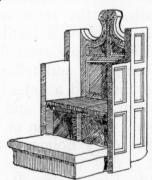

St. Augustine's Chair.

OLD LONDON

A.D. 1173

LONDON is now the biggest city in the world. In and out of London go more people every day than a few hundred years ago could have been found in the whole of England, Scotland, and Wales.

What was London like 800 years ago—in the reign of Henry. II ? A man named William Fitz-Stephen, a close friend of Becket, and one of those who saw him murdered, has written an account of it. It is the first written account that we know.

London, like other towns, was then surrounded by walls; and outside the walls to the north lay a great marsh in the place which is still called Moorfields. Beyond the walls, where now are streets, were pastures and cornfields, and streams turning the wheels of mills with a delightful noise, and woods full of game, and stags, fallow deer, boars, and wild bulls. About London was sweet, wholesome, and clear water, rising from springs or wells, streaming forth among the glistening pebble-stones. Holy Well and Clerkenwell were two of these springs.

Outside one of these gates was a smooth field or plain, now called Smithfield, where Rahere built his hospital. And there every Friday a horse-show and cattle-fair was held.

Near the centre of the city was the church of Old St. Paul's—not the one we see now. And there were also thirteen great 'abbey and convent churches, of which only one remains, that of St. Bartholomew the Great. Besides these there were a hundred and twenty-six smaller parish churches, nearly all of which were burned in the Great Fire[1] of London, 500 years later.

The Tower of London, begun by William the Conqueror, was there too, and the first stone bridge across the Thames was just then going to be built. Until then the only London Bridge was a wooden one.

Alongside the river, among wharfs and wine-stores, was a great public cook-shop where every day so much food was cooked— meat, fish and game—that, however many came to buy, there was always enough and to spare.

On feast-days and holidays the citizens came out into the playing-fields and open spaces to watch all kinds of sports: cock-

[1] See Book IV.

EARLIEST KNOWN PICTURE (FIFTEENTH CENTURY) OF
LONDON BRIDGE.

In the foreground is the Tower of London, with its white
turrets. Behind is the Bridge, with its houses. Notice
also the wharves alongside the river.

fighting, bear and bull baiting, archery,
horse-riding, and various feats of arms with
lances and shields by citizens trained for war.

In Easter week there was a sort of water-
battle on the Thames. A shield was fixed
up on a pole; and down the stream towards
the shield boats without oars were set
drifting. In the forepart of each boat stood
a young man holding a lance; and as the
boat was carried towards the shield, he struck
at it with his weapon. If the lance broke
against the shield, he had done well; but if

GROUP OF SHOPS, FIFTEENTH CENTURY.
The shop was a room which opened directly on to the street, its unglazed window being occupied by a projecting counter for displaying the wares.

the lance did not break, its pressure against the shield pushed him off into the water. And while this went on, numbers of people stood upon the bridge and wharfs, and on the roofs of houses by the river-side, and looked on and laughed.

In this story of Old London we read how a game which was perhaps the beginning of cricket—a game of bat and ball—was played. Also how in winter, when the moats and marshes were frozen, men and boys used to go sliding; and some fastened under their feet little strips of bone, by means of which,

we are told, they were able to move over the
ice " as swiftly as a bird flieth in the air, or
as an arrow from the bow."

And so we learn how even in Henry II's
reign skating had already begun.

There was dancing also, and singing,
and other music. For ever since man began
to invent anything he has invented ways of
enjoying himself.

In this picture given to us of life in a great
city 800 years ago, everything seems to have
been of the best. The only two sad things
we are told are that " idle fellows " drank
too much, and that, most of the houses being
built of wood, there were many fires in Old
London.

KING RICHARD I AND SALADIN

A.D. 1190

HENRY II was succeeded by his son Richard I, who was one of the greatest soldiers of history. Richard was very tall and strong, and was so brave that people called him " Cœur de Lion," which means the lion-heart.

When he became King he joined in the Crusades—that is, the Wars of the Cross in which Christians fought against unbelievers for the possession of the Holy Land where Our Lord lived and taught.

Richard himself went out to try and take the Holy City of Jerusalem from the followers of Mohammed, who had just retaken it. Their leader was called Saladin.

While Richard made war, he made also a great friendship with Saladin, whom he never met, and who was also his enemy. For, in those days, men so loved fighting that often they honoured greatly those against whom they fought. And so it was with King Richard and Saladin. Because they were both such brave fighters and so skilful in war, they had a warm regard for each other;

CRUSADING PICTURE (INSIDE LETTER R) SHOWING MAN IN MAIL WITH BARE LEGS, RIDING ON A HORSE (WITH FOAL BENEATH IT) FOLLOWED BY KNIGHTS IN ARMOUR.

yet each fought hard and did his best to defeat the other.

One day Richard sent word to Saladin that he greatly desired to meet him; but Saladin replied that Kings could not have speech together until they had made terms of peace; and peace was never made.

Yet when news came to Saladin that Richard was lying sick of an ague, he sent him a present of fruit, also of snow from which cooling drinks might be made to ease his fever. And when Richard was well again, and back in the field, driving the enemy from many of their strongholds, Saladin, hearing of his exploits, said: " If I am to lose this land, I would rather lose it to him than to any Prince I have ever known."

8

CRUSADING PICTURE (INSIDE LETTER B) SHOWING CRUSADERS
RETURNING FROM A RAID, WITH CATTLE AND SHEEP, AND
PRISONERS WITH BOUND HANDS AND ROPES ROUND THEIR
NECKS.

But Richard failed, in the end, to take the
Holy City; his army was not strong enough.
The story is told that one day coming to the
crest of a hill, from which the walls and
towers of Jerusalem could be seen, he turned
away his head, refusing to look at the Holy
City which he could not deliver from the
hands of the unbeliever. Not long after;
he made a three years' truce, in order that

he might go home and collect more men and money. " Then," he said, " I will return and win the whole land of Jerusalem."

But this never came to pass; for, on his way home, Richard was wrecked on the Adriatic coast; and the country through which he had to travel was ruled by a Duke who was his enemy. Richard disguised himself as a pilgrim but the Duke heard of it; and one night Richard's lodging near Vienna was surrounded, and he was carried away captive to one of the Duke's castles, where for a long while he remained a prisoner. And when at last he was set free on payment of a heavy ransom, and got back to his own kingdom, he found so much there waiting to be done, that he never had time to return to the Holy Land.

Richard was the greatest soldier of his time, and he met his death at the hands of a soldier. For one day, as he was laying siege to a castle in France, he rode too near the walls; and one of the archers defending the castle shot an arrow, which wounded him in the arm. The wound did not heal. When the castle was taken, Richard was near his death. The archer who had shot the arrow was brought to him, a prisoner.

Richard said to the man: " What evil have I done to thee ? Why hast thou slain me ?" The archer replied boldly: " Thou didst slay my father and my two brothers with thine own hand; thou wouldst have slain me likewise. Freely will I suffer the greatest torments thou canst think of, now that thou art stricken to death !"

This honest and brave answer pleased Richard. " I forgive you my death," he said, and ordered that the man should be set free.

But Richard's followers only waited till the King was dead. Then, contrary to his command, they seized the man he had pardoned, and put him to a cruel death; for the people are not always so wise as their King, nor so merciful.

INSIDE LETTER O, A MAN THROWING A STONE FROM A FORTRESS AT MAILED KNIGHTS AND ARCHERS.

THE LITTLE POOR MAN OF
ASSISI

A.D. 1182-1226

FRANCIS was the son of a rich cloth
merchant named Bernardone. As a
youth he loved singing, and dancing, and
play-acting; and because Francis's friends
came to buy his cloth, Bernardone let his
son spend most of his time in pleasure.

But one day Francis happened to be in his
father's shop, measuring cloth for a rich
customer. As he was doing so, a beggar
came by, and asked for alms in God's name.
Francis, being busy, told him to go away.

But the next moment Francis thought to
himself: " If that beggar had come to me
with a message from some great duke or
lord, I should have attended to him at once.
Why did I send him away when he came
with a message from God ?"

So, leaving his customer, he ran after the
beggar, and thanking him for his message,
put money into his hand and kissed him.

Then, leaving the beggar much astonished, he went back to his customer.

That was the beginning of a new life for Francis. He found himself called to love the poor, the weak, the sick, the oppressed. But how was he to get to them; and when he did, what was he to do ?

One thing he saw plainly: he was rich, they were poor. He made up his mind to give everything of his own to the service of God and his fellow-men.

Now his father had lately made him his partner in business. So Francis took what he thought was his own share of the cloth they had in stock, and loading his horse with it, carried it to a neighbouring town and sold it. He sold the horse also; and all the money he had received for the cloth and for the horse, he gave away in charity. He even gave away his own clothes, except those he was wearing.

When Bernardone, his father, found out what he had done, he was very angry; and because Francis had given most of his money to the Church, he summoned him before the Bishop's court, in order to get it back. The Bishop called father and son before

St. Francis.

On the right is St. Francis, who has just given his clothes to his
father and is wearing a loin-cloth; behind him stands a
bishop; to the left is the angry father.

him; and Bernardone came and told the
Bishop how his son had robbed him, selling
what was not his; and how the Church had
received money for stolen goods.

Francis was very much surprised to find
that nothing his father had given him was
really his own; even then he was wearing a
suit of clothes which he himself had not paid
for. All the rest that he had taken was gone;
but those at least he could restore.

So, going out of the court, he took off all
his clothes and made them up into a bundle.
Then, in nothing but an old shirt, he came
back and returned the clothes to his father,
who had so publicly put him to shame.
And as he did so he said the Lord's Prayer,
meaning to say that God was the only father
from whom he would henceforth ask anything.

During the rest of his life he never had
anything to call his own—except his followers, called *Friars*, a word which means
" brothers."

In due course Francis made a rule for the
brothers, by which he and they were to live:
they were to be poor, they were to have
nothing of their own; even for food and
clothes they were to depend on charity; and

they were to give work and service freely to all who asked for it.

Francis believed that those who made themselves so useful to their fellow-men, and who did it for the love of God, would be welcome wherever they went. So, going from place to place, wherever work was waiting to be done, and needing helpers, they did it. They washed dirty floors and dirty clothes, they cleaned out pig-sties, they helped at hay-making and at harvest, they rebuilt old walls, they mended shoes, they nursed the sick, they begged alms for the poor, they washed the feet of lepers.

And for all these things they never asked to be paid. A shelter for the night and enough food to keep them alive was all they hoped for; and even for that they did not ask from those to whom they gave their services.

When this work was over, they would speak to those with whom they had worked of the love of God, and would sing songs to them. And they were so happy in this kind of life which they had chosen, that people called them " Joculatores Domini," which is Latin for " God's Jesters " or " God's Players."

Ten years after Francis had formed his happy band of workers and preachers, there were thousands of them in Italy alone.

Some of the Friars came to England when Henry III was King, and were given their first lodging in Canterbury. From there they went to Oxford and other places, where homes were found for them.

Before long the Friars had carried their message of joy and free service into all parts of the known world. And all this, to begin with, came from one man, the little poor man of Assisi, St. Francis.

KING EDWARD I AND HIS
QUEEN
A.D. 1272-1307

PRINCE EDWARD, afterwards King Edward I of England, had a fair Spanish bride, called Eleanor of Castile, whose name and memory are still honoured in this country in a way that will presently be told.

While Edward was still a Prince, he left England, as Richard the Lion Heart had done, to join in the Crusades. His beautiful wife went with him; and had she not gone— if an old story is true—he might never have returned.

Prince Edward was one day in his tent, outside the city of Acre in the Holy Land. The day was hot, and the Prince was lying on a couch, unarmed, wearing a loose robe for coolness. And while he so lay, a messenger came with a letter from one of the leaders of the enemy, asking to see him.

This messenger had been to see him several times before, carrying letters to and fro between the two armies, when, as sometimes happened, they wished to stop fighting for a while.

And so, because the messenger was well known, he was taken to the tent where the Prince lay unarmed. As he entered, he bowed low, and drew out the letter which he had brought with him.

Then, as Prince Edward reached out his hand to take it, the messenger drew a dagger, sprang forward, and struck with all his might.

He had aimed at the Prince's heart; but the Prince had been too quick for him. Seeing the blow coming, he threw up his arm, wrenched the weapon from the man's hand, and the next moment had him dead.

But in the struggle the Prince had been wounded; the dagger had torn his arm, and there was poison on it. Now the poisons known to the East were so deadly that a mere scratch was often enough to cause death. So, if help had not been at hand, he might have died that same hour.

One old story tells how it was his wife Eleanor who saved him. Before the poison had time to spread, she sucked it from the wound, risking her own life for the love of him.

A VERY BEAUTIFUL EFFIGY OF QUEEN ELEANOR IN WESTMINSTER ABBEY.

The figure is in gilt bronze and has a long gown and mantle. Round the neck is a cord and on the head a crown.

But another story tells that the surgeon ordered Eleanor out of the tent, and she was led away weeping and wailing. " It is better, lady," said the bystanders, " that you should weep than the whole of England." Then, after the surgeon had done his work, the Prince rapidly got well.

Some years after, when Edward had become King and was conquering Wales, his wife, Queen Eleanor, joined him; and a son was born to them at Carnarvon Castle. When the son was sixteen he was made Prince of Wales, at a Parliament held at Lincoln, and when the people of Wales heard that news it pleased them greatly; and ever since that day the English and the Welsh have lived under one King.

Years later, when Queen Eleanor died in the north of England, the King caused her body to be brought back to London for burial in Westminster Abbey. And on the way, wherever the body rested for the night, he set up a cross to her memory. And the last resting-place of all was at Charing Cross in London, where a stone monument still stands in place of the old one which has gone.

FAMOUS STONES

IN Westminster Abbey stands one of the most famous chairs in history: the Coronation Chair, or throne, in which the Kings of this country are crowned. It was made of oak by Walter, "king's painter" to Edward I; and Walter painted pictures on it. It was also made to contain something much older—one of the famous stones of the world. This is the stone on which, in ancient times, the Kings of Scotland were crowned. Legend says that it was the stone on which Jacob slept when he dreamed his dream at Bethel, and saw the ladder of angels reaching up into Heaven.

Edward I, in one of his wars with Scotland, took this stone from the Abbey of Scone, where Scottish Kings went to be crowned, and carried it back with him to Westminster.

Now Edward I claimed also to be King of Scotland. But the Scots would never admit the claim; and, for many years after, fighting went on between the two nations, and much blood was shed. Sometimes the English were the victors, sometimes the Scots. But though the Scots were the smaller nation, they kept their own King; the English were never able to conquer them.

Then, three hundred years after King Edward I had carried away the stone, a King of Scotland became King of England, without any fighting at all. With the consent of the people of England, the Scottish King, James VI, came to Westminster; and sitting upon the ancient stone which had been taken from his own country so many years before, he was crowned as King James I of England.

After that, the King of England was always King of Scotland; and the King of Scotland was always the King of England. A hundred years later was passed a law called the " Act of Union," making the two kingdoms one, and nobody thinks of them as separate any more.

At Kingston-on-Thames, near London, is another stone on which kings are said to have been crowned. The stone stands now in the market-place. But in the old days it was kept in a church which has long since disappeared. There, a thousand years ago, some of the old Saxon Kings were crowned; and close by, the old Saxon Parliament, called the Witan, was held.

In many other places there are stones which go far back into history and once had a use and importance of their own. In a street in London can still be seen a stone called " London Stone."

One day, in the reign of King Richard II, a man named Wat Tyler came and struck the " London Stone " with his sword. He was the leader of the peasants in their great Revolt (described in a later story in this book). He struck the stone as a sign that he and his followers had taken the City of London, and would not go till the King had made them certain promises.

The " London Stone " is built into St. Swithin's Church, opposite Cannon Street Station. It is supposed to be an old Roman milestone. Possibly—like the Golden Mile-stone in the Roman Forum[1]—it was a central mark from which, through the length and breadth of our land, went Roman roads some of which we still use even today.

[1] Market-place.

THE STONE OF SCONE

H ERE'S a stone, oh, here's a stone !
 What is its story ?
To Westminster Abbey from Abbey of
    Scone,
A King brought it to set in his throne.
And now, whenever a King is crowned,
In trappings of glory, while all around
    Bells sound, and drums beat,
And a people's shout is filling the street,
    There—under the seat of his chair—
Is a silent stone, that doesn't cry out.

But in days of old, this stone, we're told,
    Had a grander story.
For on this stone, so it is said,
Coming to Bethel to make his bed,
Jacob laid his head, and dreamed
    A dream of glory: a ladder of light,
    Mounting up in the starry night;
    And up and down went angels in flight.
And a Voice was heard—or so it seemed—
By Jacob there, as he lay and dreamed—

" From thee and thy seed
Shall come salvation;
For I will make thee a mighty nation:
Through thee shall all people on earth be
    freed !"

O Stone, when our Kings to their crowning
    come,
Cry out to the Nation, and be not dumb;
" By thee and thy seed
Let all lands be freed,
That the Kingdom of God upon earth may
    come !"

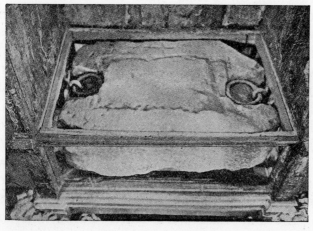

THE STONE OF SCONE—BENEATH THE CORONATION CHAIR
AT WESTMINSTER ABBEY.

GREAT TRAVELLERS

A.D. 1254-1324

ONE of the greatest travellers that the world has ever known was a man named Marco Polo. He was the son of a Venetian merchant, whose business took him to Constantinople. From that city he went trading in countries further east, going as far as Persia, about the time when Edward I was King of England.

One day Nicolo Polo, the father, while travelling in Persia with his brother, met some men who had come from Cathay, which we now call China. At that time China was under the rule of a great Emperor called Kublai Khan; and these men told Nicolo such wonderful things about the glory of their Emperor and the riches of his kingdom, that the two brothers decided to go and see them for themselves.

Now in those days nobody in Europe knew anything about China, or the people who lived there. They thought that all the races of the Far East were either barbarians or savages.

MARCO POLO'S FATHER AND UNCLE, ON THEIR FIRST JOURNEY,
KNEELING AND BEING PRESENTED TO KUBLAI KHAN.

How great, then, was the astonishment
of Nicolo and his brother when they found
themselves travelling in a land that was
more civilized than Europe—a land of vineyards, and fields, and gardens, and with
fine abbeys where monks lived, though they
were not Christian monks; and where rich
men had large houses with parks around
them, and dressed in silk, and wore clothes
covered with embroidery; and where travellers could find comfortable hotels to rest in.
It was like a fairy tale. They had not

believed that any such land, so rich and prosperous, could exist outside their own country.

Kublai Khan was as pleased to see the travellers as they were to see him, for he had never before met with any educated Europeans. He wanted to know all about Europe, and about the Christian religion.

So when at last the brothers returned home, they brought with them a letter from the Khan to the Pope, asking for a hundred teachers to be sent to China, so that the people might learn from them the religion and the arts of the Western world.

But when the brothers got back to Europe they heard that the Pope was dead; and for two years they had to wait till a new Pope was elected. But this new Pope missed a great chance, for instead of sending the hundred teachers asked for, he sent only two Friars.

When the brothers started on their second journey, they took with them Nicolo's son Marco, who was then a lad of fifteen. Going by land through Turkey, Palestine, and Persia, they crossed the Gobi Desert; and travelling with Eastern merchants who knew

KUBLAI KHAN HUNTING.

On the right you will see a stag, a wild boar, and a hind.   The
eagle, just released by Kublai Khan, is about to attack the
hind.   A hunting leopard, one of a thousand that the
Emperor kept, is sitting behind his master enjoying the hunt.
Notice also the windmill on the hill.

the way, came at last to Pekin.   The journey
had taken them three and a half years.   But
the two Friars were no longer with them;
for, after starting on the journey, they had
turned back before they got half-way.

Kublai Khan kept Marco, and his father
and uncle, for seventeen years, and made good
use of them.   In the service of the Emperor,
Marco travelled north into Siberia, where he

saw reindeer, and white bears, and fields of ice; and south into India, which was even then a rich and fertile land. He also went to Tibet, a country where no white man had ever been before, and where white men were not allowed to go again until about fifty years ago. And in order that he might travel more easily, Marco learned some of the languages that were spoken in the East.

Before white men went into those countries again, many of the beautiful things which Marco saw had disappeared; and his is the only account we have of them.

When Marco returned to Kublai Khan again, the Emperor made him governor of a large town, and wanted to keep him there always. But by this time Marco and the other two Polos had a great longing to return home; and because the Emperor had found them useful it was hard for them to get away. He did not want them to go.

But at last their chance came. For just at that time Kublai Khan was sending a Princess to be married to the King of Persia; and the three Polos were told to go with her, because they had been to Persia before and knew the country.

But this time they went not by land, but by sea. It was a long voyage; they had taken more than three years to come by land; going back by sea they took two years. When they got to Persia they found that the King, whom the Princess was to have married, had died while waiting for her, so she married one of his sons instead. But Marco and his two relatives did not go back to China, but returned to Europe, having been away more than twenty years.

When they got home to Venice they were so changed that nobody knew them. And even when they gave proof as to who they were, their friends were not pleased to see them, and found their story difficult to believe. But an old account has come down which says that, when they unstitched the padding of their coats and other garments, and showed how they were stuffed with jewels, then it was a different story; and those who had before been doubtful, became ready to welcome them, seeing that they were rich.

But even then the tales they told were so marvellous that few of them were believed; and had they not been written down for us

they would all have been lost and forgotten.

Now it so happened that Marco Polo,
fighting for his native city of Venice against
Genoa, was taken prisoner; and while in
prison, having nothing else to do, he gave
an account of his travels to a fellow-prisoner,
who wrote them all down. Some time later
these tales were published in a book, and
people at last came to believe them.

The book told them that thousands of
miles east of Europe was a very great and
rich country, worth seeing and worth trading
with.

So, partly because that book had been
written, men began making long voyages, and
trying to get to the other side of the world.
And at last some of them succeeded, and
found that the stories which Marco Polo had
told long ago were all true.

Thus it was that the travels of a peaceful
merchant and his son helped to lead to the
great days of sea-voyage and adventure, south
and east and west, and the discovery, 200
years later, of what men called " The New
World." [1]

[1] See the first story in Book IV.

A GREAT EXILE

A.D. 1265-1321

SEVEN years before Edward I became King of England, in the Italian city of Florence, a wonderful man named Dante was born. He loved his native city, even though his fellow-citizens hated him; and he loved through the whole of his life a beautiful lady named Beatrice, who died while he was still young.

In his books Dante tells us the story of his two loves: his love for the city of Florence, and his love for the lady Beatrice. He first met Beatrice when they were both nine years old. He tells us that she was dressed in dark red, richly adorned and girdled. As soon as he saw her, he loved her; his limbs trembled; and in his heart he seemed to hear these words: " Behold, a god stronger than myself has come to rule my life."

That " stronger god " was love; and he tells us how love changed him, and how out of it grew that vision of beauty which has made his name live as one of the world's greatest poets.

Dante loved Beatrice without her knowing it; we only hear of their meeting two or three times. While still young she went away and married someone else. Fifteen years after that first meeting, she died. Yet about his early love for her, and the long parting that followed, the poet Dante has told one of the most beautiful stories that was ever written.

Dante's love for his city makes an even sadder story than his love for Beatrice. For at that time the people of Florence were divided into two parties, called the Whites and the Blacks. It came from an old quarrel between two families, which had gone on for many years. Dante belonged to one of these parties, and had helped to govern the city while his party was in power. When the other party came back to power again, he, with many others, was driven away into exile. In his absence, he was condemned to pay a heavy fine, and deprived of the right to hold public office for the rest of his life. All his property was seized; and when he did not return, he and fourteen others were condemned to be burned alive if ever again they set foot in Florence.

Dante never saw his native city again. Years afterwards he might have got leave to return, had he been willing to pay the fine demanded of him, and do penance for what he had done. But as Dante had done nothing wrong, he would not do these things, and he was an exile till the day of his death.

So Florence, one of the most famous places in history, is remembered also as the city which drove into exile the greatest man who was ever born there. In Florence there is a stone called " Dante's Chair," because tradition says that, while he lived in Florence, he used often to sit on it. And because of Dante, that stone seat is still held in high honour, and people come to look at it. But for the last twenty years of his life Dante never once sat there. All those years he remained an exile, his heart filled with longing for his two lost loves—his lady Beatrice, and Florence, his native city.

A story is told that late one dark night, knocking was heard at the door of a monastery among the mountains of Italy. The porter went, and opening the small gate-

HERE IS DANTE HAVING HIS PORTRAIT PAINTED BY GIOTTO, THE GREATEST ARTIST OF HIS DAY.

This portrait still exists in Italy.

window, peeped out to see who was there. In the darkness he saw two bright burning eyes fixed on him. " What do you want ?" he asked, rather frightened, after he had waited a while for the other to speak. " Peace !" answered a voice. It was Dante; and turning away he vanished into the night.

All his life Dante was looking for peace; in the world of his fellow-men he never found it. But in the long sorrow of his exile he wrote his great poem, " The Divine Comedy," as it is called; a wonderful vision of life in the next world, as men then believed it to be. The last poem, about Paradise, he finished just before he died. In that poem he meets Beatrice again, and she becomes his guide. By gazing into her eyes he is lifted into the beauty of Paradise; and through her smile he reads the meaning of things in Heaven.

In one passage of the poem he tells how Beatrice in Paradise turns and looks at the sun. And because she, whom he so loves, looks at it with clear eyes, he himself is able to see the sun more clearly than ever before. But it seems to him a different sun from the sun he knew on earth; its light has a new meaning for him, such as it never had before.

So the story comes round. The same thing happens to him in his last years as when he was a child of nine. " Behold, a god stronger than myself has come to rule my life," was the thought that came to him as a child, when he and Beatrice first met. And now, at the end, it is Beatrice who is still teaching him to know the true life.

Here are two Drawings of Dante Meeting Beatrice, one on Earth (Left), and one in Paradise (Right).

HOW A QUEEN SAVED NOBLE LIVES

A.D. 1346

EDWARD III, grandson of Edward I and son of Edward II, who at the age of sixteen had been made Prince of Wales, was at war with France. For almost a year he had been trying to take the city of Calais. All that time the citizens had held out, hoping that the French King could save them. But at the end of eleven months the people were starving, and no hope was left.

So, when the people found that they must give up the city, they feared that all might have to die; and they sent to ask the English King for terms of mercy. Edward said he would spare their lives if they would give him six of their chief men to do with as he liked; and they were to come barefoot, each man in nothing but his shirt, and with a rope round his neck.

Now, when the people of Calais heard this news, there was great grief; and many wondered whether six men could be found willing to die for the rest.

THE BURGHERS OF CALAIS.

The Queen has not yet arrived But notice the King on the left, and the Burghers on the right with ropes round their necks, and the walls of Calais beyond.

But without waiting for names to be chosen, a great merchant named Eustace St. Pierre, the richest of all the men of Calais, offered to be the first. After him came five others. So these six men, amid the tears and blessings of the people they were now going to save, went out of the city, and were taken into the King's presence.

Then Eustace, speaking for the rest, knelt at the King's feet and offered their lives to his will, but begged him of his goodness to have mercy on them.

But King Edward III, full of wrath because the city had so long held out against him, refused their prayer, and gave word for them to be put to death. Then one of his own knights, Sir Walter de Manny, pleaded for them, begging the King to do a gentle deed, and win honour and fame by granting pardon to men so noble and so brave.

But this only made the King more angry. " Hold your peace, Sir Walter !" he cried. " These men of Calais have killed many of mine, and they must die too."

Then must it have seemed that their death was certain. But at the King's side sat his wife, Queen Philippa; and she, in spite of

the King's wrath against his own good knight,
took up the prayer and made it her own.
Throwing herself at his feet, she begged him
by the love he had for her, and for the many
dangers and hardships she had borne in
coming from England to be with him, and
above all for the love of Christ, that he would
now show mercy and spare these men their
lives

The King looked at her for awhile without
speaking, for he was a man whose mind was
always hard to change. Then said he:
" Lady, I would rather that you had not
come here at all; for you know how to pray
in such manner that I dare not refuse. But
though I do it against my will, I put their
lives in your hands."

And so saying, he took the six men by the
ropes which were round their necks, and
gave them to the Queen.

Then, with tears of joy, Queen Philippa
thanked the King for his mercy; and loosing
them from their bonds, she gave orders for
them to be well clothed and fed, and sent
them back safe and alive to their own city.

A KING'S PITY

" GO out ! Go out, ye six doomed men.
      Go out, and save the city !
Go out, and come not back again;
   And Christ on your souls have pity !"

Forth went six, all doomed to die,
   That their city might be forgiven;
With a hangman's rope to lift them high
   To the dark gates of Heaven.

The scaffold was set, and doom was said,
   And the six ropes hung ready;
And each, with a city's price on his head,
   Under the rope stood steady.

But a light from Heaven on earth was seen,
   For the men that had saved their city:
Christ came into the heart of a Queen,
   And taught a King to have pity.

" Go back ! go back, ye living men,
   And ring the bells of your steeple !
And let the tale be told again,
   How pity has blessed a people."

THE BURGHERS OF CALAIS

CHARACTERS

EDWARD III, *King of England.*
PHILIPPA, *his Queen.*
SIR WALTER MANNY.
LORD STAFFORD.
SIR BARTHOLOMEW BURGHERSH.
EUSTACE DE ST. PIERRE.
FIVE BURGHERS OF CALAIS.
KNIGHTS, LORDS, SOLDIERS, HERALDS, TRUM-
PETERS, and ATTENDANTS.

> *In the English camp outside the walls of
> Calais, in front of the King's tent, is an open
> space surrounded by barriers. Outside the
> barriers are troops standing under arms.
> Before the entrance of the tent stands a dais;
> round about are* LORDS *and* KNIGHTS. *Re-
> tainers enter; at their head is a* HERALD, *with
> two* TRUMPETERS. *The trumpets sound.*

HERALD. Oyez! The King!

> [*The* KING *enters, accompanied by the* QUEEN,
> *followed by* LORDS. *He mounts the dais.*]

KNIGHTS (*saluting*). God bless and keep your
Grace!

KING. Aye, surely, so He has! This day
crowns all:
Calais surrenders.

QUEEN. To your mercy.

KING. To my justice.

QUEEN. Let them be one, my lord! For noble
hearts,
Surely, that is not hard!

KING. War is war, lady. But I *have* shown
mercy.
Is't not great mercy to let six men die,
That Calais may be spared? Most guilty
Calais!

QUEEN. Oh, now you speak a different tongue,
my lord,
To that which wooed me.

KING. Aye! With enemies
I speak as they shall know. . . . Are they
not come?

SIR WALTER MANNY. Not yet, my lord.

KING. 'Tis time. Come they not now—
Sound, and storm down the city: wait no
more!
If they keep not their word, then Calais
dies!

STAFFORD. My lord, they come !

> [*Toward the barriers advance the six* BURGHERS *of Calais, led by* EUSTACE DE ST. PIERRE. *They come in sackcloth, heads bare, and with ropes round their necks.*]

SIR WALTER. Dead men ! Look ! Oh, 'tis brave

The way they march !—Their goal a felon's death.

See how they face it !

STAFFORD. Aye ! nobly, indeed !

KING. Open the barriers there ; and let them in !

> [*The barriers are opened. The* BURGHERS *enter, and kneel.*]

BURGHERSH. 'Tis done, my lord. The citizens are here.

They wait your pleasure.

KING. Bring them !

> [BURGHERSH *goes, and by a gesture bids them rise. They all rise together as one man, and stand erect.*]

SIR WALTER.   Oh ! my lord.

Look, look ! Shall these men die, that come to it

So brave and willing ?

KING. Surely, saving others,
Could men die better ?

QUEEN. Oh, why should others die ?
Why any ?

KING. Peace ! Enough, enough ! No more.

EUSTACE. Dread King, by these commanded
hands, to you
Calais her keys surrenders, and her walls,
Weapons, and wealth, and all her people's
lives,
Praying your mercy.

KING. These truly are the keys ?

EUSTACE. My lord, our city
Lies there before you. All the gates stand
open :
Within, a starving people—half are dead.
Were more lives left—had *we* more life and
strength—
We would not now be pleading.

SIR WALTER. Bravely said !

STAFFORD. Not wisely.

SIR WALTER. Oh, surely a King can hear
Kingliness spoken !

KING. Well, you know what price
You pay us for our mercy ?

9*

EUSTACE. Aye, my lord !
These ropes upon our necks speak as to that
All that needs saying.

KING. Why, then, well said, indeed !
Your errand done, demands no further
answer.
We pass from words to deeds. . . .
Take forth the prisoners, and strike off their
heads.

STAFFORD. He spares them hanging !

SIR WALTER. I had hoped for more.

QUEEN (*kneeling*). My lord, oh, let me speak,
now let me speak !

KING. How now ?

QUEEN. These men are noble ! And being what
they are,
They deserve not to die ! And I deserve,
Being as I am—that you should grant my
prayer !
Nay ! hear me still !
Myself will of their ransoms pay a part;
And here be also others, that are willing,
Or shall be, when I ask them ! Speak, my
lords !

SEVERAL. My lord, we are, we are !

QUEEN.   Ah, gentle sir,
    Since I have crossed the sea, to my own
       danger,
    To bring you comfort, never have I asked
    One favour of your love. But now I ask it
    That—for Christ's sake, and having love
       for me,
    You will be merciful to these six men !

KING. Ah, lady, for such words I must do
       deeds.
    I would you had been anywhere but here !
    You have entreated me in such a manner
    That I cannot refuse you.   These six men
    I give you them, to do with as you please.

QUEEN. A gift, my lord—their worth being what
       it is—
    Worthy of him that gives it ! Thanks, my
       lord !
    What words can say not, life from me shall
       show
    Oh, you have blessed its day ! (*To the*
       BURGHERS) Sirs, God has saved you !
    (*To the* BYSTANDERS). Run, some of you,
       and tell the citizens
    Their lives are spared !   And you, sirs, come
       with me !

You shall be clothed, and fed.   We'll make
a feast.

You must be hungry.

[*She goes in, followed by* BURGHERS *and*
ATTENDANTS.]

KING. Look you, my lords ! And say not that
the Heavens
Have shut their ancient use.   For ye have
seen
Descend to earth this day, manna from
Heaven.

SIR WALTER. God bless your lady, and you also,
sir.

KING. He has done so abundantly already,
And more—as time shall show !   Come, let's
move on !
Sound trumpets, and set forward to the city.
We bring them peace.

[*The trumpets sound ; the troops form ranks
and march.*]

THE PEASANTS' REVOLT

A.D. 1381

WHEN King Richard II, the grandson of Edward III, was still only a boy, the peasants of England rose in revolt, and marched upon London.

The peasants thought they had many grievances; and all through the country there was discontent.

Then, in the country of Kent, there arose a popular preacher named John Ball, who said things would never be well in England till all worked and laboured alike, and rich and poor were equal. Word of his preaching went to other places; and because of the discontent, many became his followers.

So out of the home counties, Kent and Essex and Sussex, the peasants came marching toward London, sixty thousand strong. And they had as their leader a man named Wat Tyler, who had fought in the French wars; and with him was another man of the people named Jack Straw, and the priest John Ball.

Some of the rebels came upon London

from the north side of the Thames, and some from the south; and as they marched through the country they pillaged and burned the homes of the rich, and hanged all the lawyers they could lay hands on.

The men of Kent even sacked the palace of the Archbishop of Canterbury at Lambeth; then, forcing their way across London Bridge, they entered the city, and burned the house of the King's uncle, John of Gaunt; and driving out the lawyers from their abode called the Temple, destroyed all the records of their services which they found there. " It was marvellous to see," says the chronicler, " how even the most aged and infirm of lawyers scrambled off with the agility of rats."

For three whole days the city was held by the rebels with riot, uproar, and feasting; and so strong were they that none could turn them out.

All that time the King was with his court in the Tower of London, which stood at one end of the city; and outside were fields. Then the King, though he was but a boy, said that he would go and meet the rebels, at a place outside the walls called Mile End,

JOHN BALL, ON A HORSE, PREACHING.

Notice the Royal Standard, made up half of the Arms of England, half of the Arms of France.

and would there hear all they had to complain about. This he did; and between them they made an agreement. The people asked, by their leaders, that they should all become free men and not be bondmen any more. And the King promised that, if they would go back to their homes and villages, he would do as they asked him, and would send after them writings, sealed in the King's name, granting all their demands.

But while the King was thus making terms with the rebels at Mile End, the other rebels within the city, under Wat Tyler, had seized the Tower itself, and killed the Archbishop and the King's Treasurer; and the whole city remained as before in the hands of the rebels. So the next day the King arranged to meet Wat Tyler himself. Coming from Westminster Abbey, where he had first gone to hear Mass, he went to Smithfield. There, in front of the Abbey Church of St. Bartholomew, which Rahere had built, he came on Wat Tyler, who had with him a strong body of armed rebels.

As soon as Wat Tyler saw the King arriving with his lords, he rode forward to meet him; and speaking to him very much as an equal, man to man, he made the same demands for his followers as had been made the day before at Mile End, by the men coming from Essex. And the King gave them the same answer, that he would see to it, and that all should be done.

But among the King's followers were some who were angered by the rudeness with which Wat Tyler spoke to the King. And one of them, William Walworth, Lord Mayor of London, riding up to him, struck him across the head with a sword, and brought him to the ground. Then one of the King's squires sprang down from horse and stabbed him before he had time to rise.

The armed crowd, seeing their leader thus slain before their eyes, bent their bows and made ready to fight. And they so many, and the King's party so few, there was danger then that none of the King's men might escape alive. But the King, though only a boy, did a wise and brave thing. All alone, he rode out to meet them. " Men, what are ye about ?" he cried. " Ye shall have me for your Captain—me ! I am your King: keep peace !"

These words of the young King won the

hearts of the people. They gave up possession of the city and returned to their homes

The King, because the lords in Parliament
did not agree, was unable to keep his
promises. But though the revolt failed,
the old ways were slowly changing, and in
time the peasants of England ceased altogether
to be bondmen to those who held the land.

RICHARD II ADDRESSING REBELS.

On the left is the Lord Mayor of London striking Wat Tyler
with a sword, and behind Wat Tyler is King Richard.
On the right the King is addressing the rebels after
Wat Tyler's death.

JOAN OF ARC

A.D. 1429

JOAN OF ARC, the Maid of France, lived in a village called Domremy. Her father was a farmer in a small way; and Joan used to go into the fields to look after the sheep. She was also good at business, and helped her father to keep his accounts; but she must have done this in her head, for she could not read or write.

Yet this peasant girl, when only seventeen, became the leader of an army. She helped France to win back its freedom from the English, who had been fighting in France, off and on, from the time of Edward III (as we saw in the story of Calais).

That is a marvellous thing for a young girl to have done; no wonder her name became famous.

Now whenever Joan was in doubt about what to do, she said she used to hear Voices speaking to her. The Voices always told her right; and as everything they told her was good, she was sure that they came from God.

At this time the northern part of France was ruled by the English King, who claimed the French throne. Even Paris itself, and Rheims, the city where the French Kings were always crowned, were under English control. So France had two Kings; one was French, the other was foreign. And Charles, the French King, had not yet been crowned, because he could not get to Rheims. Now Charles was a man of weak will, and rather feeble mind. And because he greatly disliked war and fighting, he did nothing to make good his claim to the crown of France. So the French had become disheartened, and had almost given up hope of freeing their land from the foreigners.

That was how things were when Joan formed her plan for saving France. The English at that time were besieging Orleans. The siege had lasted many months, and the city would soon have to surrender if help did not come. The French were quarrelling among themselves, and had no one to lead them, so nothing was done.

Now Joan was eager and active, and full of courage. She loved France dearly. Time passed. One day she again heard the Voices speaking to her, and saying, "Go into France, save Orleans, and lead the King to be crowned at Rheims." Joan had thought she heard the Voices say much the same thing while she was still a child; but this time the message was so plain that she dared not resist. Yet it seemed an impossible thing to do. Even to get speech with the King— she a poor peasant girl, and he heir to the throne—would be hard enough. But without waiting to count the difficulties, she set out.

She began by getting her uncle to take her to one of the King's officers, a man of high rank.

When the officer heard what she had come about, he told her uncle to box her ears and take her home again. Somehow she persuaded the officer that she was not mad but was talking sense. He gave her a horse and a sword, and she put on man's clothes as better for travelling. After riding for two weeks by night, so as to avoid capture by the English soldiers in search of supplies, she came to King Charles's court, and sent him her message.

At first the King refused to see her or

believe that her message meant anything. Then, as a test, he disguised himself, and making another take the chief place, he stood among a crowd of courtiers. But Joan, on coming into the court, picked him out from among them all, and repeated her message to him alone.

Many of those standing by must have laughed to hear a poor peasant girl say that she had come to save France, and crown Charles as King. Charles himself doubted. She was asked to give a sign that what the Voices had told her was true. She said: "My sign shall be that I will free Orleans from its besiegers. Send many or few to help me, and God will give us the victory."

She spoke so confidently that she got the King to believe her, or at least to let her try what she could do. He put a large body of troops under her command, and she set out for Orleans.

Word went before her that a woman, who had promised them victory, was leading the French army. In those days people were more ready to believe in wonders and witchcraft than they are now. The English became frightened; the defenders of Orleans

THE TAKING OF ORLEANS BY JOAN OF ARC.

full of hope. Whatever the cause, the English were driven back from Orleans, and the city was saved. Other cities also opened their gates to her; wherever she went, the English retreated before her.

Then Joan returned in haste to the King, and led him in triumph to Rheims, where he was crowned King of France.

And now that the work to which the Voices had called her was done, she asked to be allowed to go home again, and look after her father's sheep.

But the soldiers loved her too well, and wished no one else to lead them; and the newly-crowned King, seeing that there was still a use for her, would not let her go.

So Joan remained with the army. But she was no longer allowed to do the things she wished to do. She was a much better leader than the men whose orders she had now to obey; many mistakes were made, much time was lost, and things began to go badly again. She still gained victories, and took towns from the enemy; but most of what she won for her own side was lost again by bad leadership. And then one day, at the crossing of a river, she and a small body of men were attacked by a stronger force of the enemy, and Joan was taken prisoner.

The rest of her story is very sad. Her captors were men of Burgundy, allies of the English, and to the English they sold her.

She was accused of being a false prophetess, and was brought before a Church court, presided over by a French bishop, on a charge of heresy and witchcraft. After being kept in prison for many months, and brought to trial and condemned, she was tied to a stake in the market-place of Rouen, and there burned.

To the end she was full of faith and courage. " My Voices *were* of God !" she said, in answer to her judges, who tried to throw doubt on them. As she died, men heard her calling on the name of Christ; and filled with fear at what they had done, " We have killed a saint !" they said.

A few years later another trial was held to examine once more into the charges which had been made against her. And though the second trial could not restore her to life, it gave clear proof of her innocence.

Nobody now thinks of Joan of Arc as a witch. Not many years ago the Roman Church declared her to be a Saint; and her memory is loved and honoured today just as much by the English nation as by the French.

THE FIRST ENGLISH
PRINTER

A.D. 1476

IN the old days all books were manuscript, which means " written by hand." Men spent their lives copying them; a single copy was sometimes the work of months. Books were rare and hard to come by. In monasteries and colleges, libraries of books were to be found; but, even in the houses of rich men, books were few. People did not read as they do now; and only a few could write.

Then, because the writing of books took so long, and copies were always being wanted, someone invented a way of making copies by what was called " block-printing." On a block of wood, the size of the page, a whole page of writing was cut by an engraver. If the book had a hundred pages, a hundred engraved blocks were made and used in the printing of it. The engraving of the blocks took a long time; but as soon as the blocks were made, hundreds of copies could be printed. In this way time was saved, but the labour was great.

This kind of printing was used in China hundreds of years before—even before Marco Polo travelled there; but it did not come to be used in Europe till the beginning of the fifteenth century.

Then somebody thought of a better way still; and the printers began making separate letters which could be moved about, and used for more than one book. Of every single letter in the alphabet they made hundreds of copies, from moulds cast in metal; and by arranging these they set up books word by word, in lines and pages— just as we have them now; and from these they printed as many copies as were needed.

Printing of this kind began in Europe, first perhaps in the city of Mainz on the Rhine, about the middle of the fifteenth century. About twenty years later it was brought into England, and the first English book was printed at Westminster in 1476, when Edward IV was reigning.

Who introduced it ? A man named William Caxton. He was the first English printer.

Caxton did not begin life as a printer. He was born somewhere in the Weald of

Kent. Of his boyhood he says: "I am bounden to pray for my father's and mother's souls, that in my youth sent me to school, by which, by the sufferance of God, I am getting my living, I hope, truly."

Caxton became the apprentice of a London merchant; and when his master died he left

A WRITER, OR SCRIBE, OF THE MIDDLE AGES.

England for Bruges, and he remained in the Low Countries for some thirty years. He obtained a business of his own, and became prosperous.

For a time he was in the household of the Duchess of Burgundy; and while at her court, he met and found favour with her brother, our King Edward IV, who had been driven out of England by his enemies. Very soon, however, King Edward returned to his throne; and a year or two later, Caxton followed him to England.

In the Low Countries Caxton had seen the new way of book-printing, and had learned the trade. He began translating books into English, and printing them. Until then nearly all the books which came into England were printed in French or Latin. But now, with Caxton, English printing began of books written in English. Among the books that he printed, one of the most famous was Chaucer's *Canterbury Pilgrims*, the story of which has already been told.

Caxton's house and workshop were made known to visitors by his sign of the Red Pale —a shield marked with a red bar down the middle. By this sign he invited buyers to the press, which he set up near the west front of the Abbey in the Almonry at Westminster, the place where the alms of the Abbey were given to the poor.

Now it was only after books were printed that more people—other than priests, monks and scholars—began learning to read. A hundred years later, in many of the churches, chained Bibles and other sacred books had been placed, so that the people who could not afford to buy books might read them. In Wimborne Minster a whole row of these chained books can still be seen; but nobody reads in them now, because printing and paper have become so cheap that all who wish can have books of their own.

AN EARLY PRINTING PRESS (1520).

On the right, setting type by hand; in the centre, taking an impression; on the left, preparing the ink. On the table a pile of printed sheets, and a pile of clean sheets ready for printing.

FIELD AND TOWN: THEN
AND NOW

FOR each man, woman, boy or girl who was alive in England 500 years ago, there are *ten* to-day. All these extra people live in towns. Indeed, though there are now ten times as many people as there were then, there are fewer of them in the villages !

The new great towns of to-day are not like the old ones; and in many of them a boy would have to walk many hours before he would find a farm. In these new towns boys and girls grow up to be men and women who have never seen a plough working, or a man sowing corn, or a cow being milked. In the old days this was all different. Except perhaps in London, towns were so small that it was often a rule that the town people might be called on to help get in the corn harvest ! The town was just a big village.

Thus, to understand the life of the Middle Ages, we have to remember what a large part of it was made up of country life. So here, instead of a story, is a picture showing what a farm was like in those days. This picture was made in the Low Countries, when Caxton, the first English printer, was still living there.

In the foreground is a team of horses ploughing, and just beyond it is a horse drawing a harrow, and a peasant sowing corn.

To the left is a group of peasants working among the vineyards and the orchards, where men are pruning and cutting off branches.

To the right a peasant and his wife are looking after the cattle, horses, pigs, and sheep.

In the background are the house and out-buildings of the lord of the manor. Near by can be seen the bees which gave the honey to sweeten things before sugar was discovered and brought to Europe. Notice that the painter has made the bees rather large, so that you should not miss seeing them, as they leave their hives and start to fly over the buildings.

In all these old things we see little difference from the farm-labour of our own day, so long as it is still done by hand and not by machinery. A ploughman of the Middle Ages would understand the meaning of a

COUNTRY LIFE ABOUT FIVE HUNDRED YEARS AGO.

10

plough as it is made today; he would recognize the fields and the furrows, the stables and the beehives.

In the villages and little towns of old England, people seldom moved more than a mile or so from their homes. They all knew each other and were mostly cousins. The village was like a large family where it was no use anyone pretending to be greater or richer than he was, for everyone knew how much money he had, who his father was, and what sort of fellow he had been since a child.

But now the towns are so big, and the people have to scatter so far from their work, that neighbours often know nothing of each other. And though there are crowds in the streets, yet life can be very lonely.

In the Middle Ages, houses in towns were more beautiful than they are to-day. One reason is that rich merchants had little to spend their money on, except to build fine homes and fill them with beautiful furniture and silver. They were very fond, too, of building churches, often larger than there were people to fill them. Some did this for the glory of God, and others just because they were proud.

The rich men were mostly those who owned great flocks of sheep and sold the wool. English wool was so good, and sold so well, that the sheep were spoken of as the Golden Hoof. Wool merchants would hang a Golden Fleece over the shop. Then the wool would be given out to the villagers to spin and weave, and it was very profitable. There are many villagers where the biggest old house and the church were both built by the wealthy clothier.

Life was more merry in the villages then. The Church had many joyful Saints' Days, which were Holy Days, or holidays. There were Miracle Plays in the churches, and the Maypole and dancing on the village green. There were many market-days when people met each other and sold and gossiped. Once a year, towards the autumn, at a fixed place in the county, would be *the* big fair to which all the countryside came to buy goods for the winter. It was great fun, with jugglers and wrestlers and dwarfs and giants and boxing and wrestling. But there were many cruel sights, such as bear-baiting and bull-baiting, when dogs and bears and other animals were set to fight each other.

There was also the constant fear of dreadful diseases; for terrible forms of plague, and what we now call smallpox, killed most of the children before they grew up. No one had any idea what to do. But about 150 years ago doctors came to know more, and ever since so many more children have grown up that there are now ten times as many people in England as in the old days.

Steam and electricity and motors have made the towns to-day larger than we want them to be. But these same things have made it possible in recent years for 100,000 people to leave the slums of London. They live now in the greatest garden city in the world, among the fields of Essex.

In our great towns and factories the change is so great that no one coming from the Middle Ages would understand what they meant. Nor have we in our towns yet learned to do what the men of the Middle Ages did so well—to make towns beautiful.

We want to see the factories moving into the country. Then the workers will be near their work and have the joys of the country as well as the comforts of the town.

For electricity is coming to the villages to

light and to cook, to sweep carpets and pump the water, to let us talk on the telephone and to listen to the wireless.

Perhaps, if we are sensible, we are going to be happier than we have ever been before. But we have not yet built the Fair City. And that is what we must learn to do.

MONTH OF JULY IN LATER MIDDLE AGES.

In the foreground is a man on horseback, with his dogs, and with a falcon on his wrist, preceded by another man also with a falcon. In the middle are two peasants making hay. In the background is the manor house.

THE FAIR CITY

(A Summer Day's Dream)

LET'S build the fair city! And how
shall we build it?
It shall not need ramparts to keep out the
foe;
We'll fill it with houses, and when we have
filled it,
We'll give it wide gates for the people to go.

And be the streets narrow, or be the streets
wide,
Let the windows be large, giving plenty of
light;
Let the houses have drains and good gutters
outside,
And let there be lamps in the street all the
night.

Across the broad river let bridges be built;
And let churches abound with abundance of
bells;

And into the river no dust shall be spilt.
The streets must be clean, and there mustn't
   be smells.

The air shall be clear and unsmutted by
   smoke,
And dirty-brown fogs shall be things of the
   past;
And there shall not be people who think it
   a joke
To run up the death-rate by driving too fast.

There shall not be factions, there shall not be
   fights,
There shall not be any too poor or too rich;
Nor anyone cheated and robbed of his rights,
Nor any lame dog left to die in the ditch.

A court for King's justice, a court for the
   King,
And parks and green places for people to
   play;
And once every week we'll have bell-ringers
   ring,
And bathing and bands in the park every
   day.

And all through the town shall be trees in
　the high streets,
Where lamplight shall gleam through a
　flutter of leaves;
And round them so kindly and quiet the
　bye-streets,
That swallows will come there and build in
　the eaves.

Oh, give us a city, with goods to deliver
Like that, and the song of the world going
　by;
With boat-song and music of reeds from
　the river,
And folk-song, and scaling of bells from the
　sky.

Yes, give us that city and we will live in it,
And deck it with dances, and sound it with
　song;
And word shall go forth from the dwellers
　within it,
" How fair is the city to which we belong !"

COLUMBUS DISCOVERS "THE NEW WORLD"

A.D. 1492

FIVE hundred years ago the people of Europe did not even know that America existed. Ships in those days did not go far from land; traders kept to the coast. So what we now call the Atlantic Ocean was never crossed, and nobody knew what lay on the other side.

People knew that far away, to the east and south of Asia, lay India and Cathay (as China was called), which Marco Polo[1] had visited in the thirteenth century. To get to those lands of ancient wealth men had to go long journeys full of danger and difficulty— journeys which took many months, and some- times years. Going by sea would be much quicker and much easier.

But men already knew that the world was round. And so it seemed certain that, if they were to sail far enough west, they would come to Asia—to India and Cathay—the other way round, and so find a new route to the East.

[1] See page 244 of this series.

All this had been thought of for a long time; but nobody had dared to attempt so great an adventure, nor had anyone made plans for it; for nobody could be found willing to face the heavy cost, at so large a risk.

Then there came into the world a man named Christopher Columbus, who not only wanted to do it, but made up his mind that he would do it, however great the difficulty might be.

Columbus was a native of Genoa, one of the great seaports of Italy. He was the son of a cloth-weaver; but at the age of fourteen he went to sea, and became a trader, sailing on merchant ships to all parts of the Mediterranean.

How long Columbus followed his trade from Genoa we do not know; but from early years he had looked forward and planned for the great adventure which was to make his name famous; and while still a young man he left Genoa and came to Portugal.

The Portuguese were at that time a great seafaring nation: they had made many voyages of discovery along the coast of Africa; and about that time one of their sea-captains succeeded in doubling what is now called the Cape of Good Hope. Twelve years later the greatest of their explorers, Vasco da Gama,

COLUMBUS AND THE EGG.
See the play which follows for this famous story.

discovered the sea-route to India and the Far
East, by going round Africa and across the
Indian Ocean; but that was not done till after
Columbus had made his great discovery in
the Far West.

So it was to Portugal that Columbus first
came with the plans he had made so long and
so carefully. He hoped to find there some
person of wealth and power who would be
willing to provide the ships, the money, and
the men, which he himself could not do.

Getting no help in Portugal, he went on to Spain; and there at last, after long waiting and many disappointments, success came to him. With the help of a few true friends, who had heard his plan and believed in it, he was brought to the Court of Queen Isabella of Castile and her husband Ferdinand. He told Queen Isabella of his plan, and he told it so confidently and well, that she believed it to be really possible, and promised that she would help him. It was a brave offer, but it was also a wise one; for if, indeed, this great discovery was ever to be made, the Queen might well wish that her own country of Spain should have the wealth and power and glory that would come from it.

Yet even now the long waiting was not over; for though she had promised him help, Queen Isabella could not at once find the means. For another six years Columbus waited, and was almost in despair. He had even made up his mind to leave Spain and try his fortune in France, when the Queen sent for him again, and without further delay provided all that was necessary for three ships, with crew, arms, and provisions, to start out on that most famous of all voyages of discovery.

Columbus had waited for eighteen years; and during that time, grief and hardship and disappointment had turned his hair quite grey; though only forty-six, he already looked almost like an old man.

The expedition set out from Spain on August 3rd, 1492, and Columbus was appointed its Admiral. This was seven years after Henry VII became King of England.

The ship in which Columbus sailed was called the *Santa Maria*; it had the Christian cross on its sails, and above the mainmast flew the flag of Castile. For those days it was reckoned a large ship, but we should have thought it a very small one for so long a voyage, and especially for a voyage which was going to take not days but months.

So Columbus, sailing himself in the *Santa Maria*, and with two other ships under his command, left Spain for the far and unknown West.

But it was not till a month later, when they had touched at the Canary Islands, and left them again, that the real dangers and difficulties of their adventure began. For now they were sailing into an unknown sea. And day followed day, and week followed week;

and smooth seas and favourable winds carried them further and further from home. Had they now wanted to turn back, with the wind so set to the westward, they could not have done so. The crew began to fear that the wind, so favourable to their present course, might prevent them from ever returning. The further they went, the greater became their fear. They wanted to go no further.

Then, one day, the wind changed and blew against them from the west. And because the wind had changed for a while, showing that return was possible, the crew recovered their courage and agreed to go on.

But when a month had gone by, and still no land, the seamen again lost heart. The crews of the three ships and most of the officers grew frightened, and wanted to turn back; and when Columbus refused, they grew angry as well.

And at last, though he was their captain, they threatened no longer to obey him, and said that if he would not himself give the order to return, they would choose a captain in his place and take the ship back themselves.

Very likely they would soon have done so, but the next day something happened which gave

COLUMBUS LANDING IN ONE OF THE ISLANDS WHICH HE
DISCOVERED IN HIS FIRST VOYAGE.

Notice in the top half of picture the three ships, and the natives
fleeing; and in the lower half, the Cross being erected,
Columbus and his two soldiers, and the natives bringing
presents.

them hope. Past one of the ships floated a
few green rushes, a cane, and a pole. And
then out of the water one of the seamen picked
a small stick with marks on it cut by a knife.
These things meant surely that land was near.

The hopes of the crews revived; a rich
reward had been offered for the first who
should see land; and that night a sharp look-
out was kept from all the three ships.

But the first thing seen was not land at all.
It was a dark night; the moon had not yet
risen, when Columbus, standing on the poop
of his ship, saw far out ahead a light that
moved. He called to him one of the crew,
who also saw it. Twice afterwards Columbus
saw it again, and each time he saw it the light
seemed to move. He was sure now that
where there was a light there was land. The
next day land was sighted.

Yet it was not Cathay or India that they had
reached; without knowing it, they had come
upon a New World, which we now call
America. But the land they sighted and
visited was not America itself, but an island in
the Gulf of Mexico. Yet in the finding of that
island the discovery of America had begun.

But all his life Columbus thought that he
had reached the Indies by finding a new way
to them, which was what he had set out to
do. And that is why those islands off the
American coast are called the " West Indies,"
and why the natives of America are called
" Red Indians," though they have nothing
whatever to do with the real India of Asia.

It was not till after Columbus' death that
the name " America " was given to that New

World which Columbus had really discovered without knowing it. By that discovery, so much greater than he knew, he made himself one of the world's most famous men.

THE "SANTA MARIA."

A model of the ship in which Columbus sailed on the voyage which led to the discovery of America. It has three masts, a high poop and forecastle, a rounded bow, and square stern. The white flag on the foremast has a green cross, the badge of the Band of Discoverers. On the mainmast is the Royal Standard of Castile. The length of the ship was 95 feet, the breadth $25\frac{1}{2}$ feet, and the displacement, when fully laden, 233 tons.

AN EGG, AND ITS MASTER

In a chamber of the Palace of the Queen of Spain, GENTLEMEN OF THE COURT *are gathered for a meal which stands ready waiting, with servers in attendance. Cloaks and hats are being laid aside.*

1ST GENTLEMAN. Well, Señors,[1] we are all here, are we not ? Let us sit down.

2ND GENTLEMAN (*drily*). All but " the Great Man." He is late.

3RD GENTLEMAN. " The Great Man ?" Oh ! Columbus ? Well, Columbus was but the son of a cloth-weaver. Why should we, who are of noble birth, wait for *him* ?

4TH GENTLEMAN. The son of the cloth-weaver is now an Admiral, Señor. Also, we must not forget, he discovered the New Way to the East for us.

3RD GENTLEMAN. Well, someone *had* to discover it.   It just happened to be he.

---

[1] Pronounce ' senyors.'

4TH GENTLEMAN. Yes, Señor; because he happened also to be a great man.

2ND GENTLEMAN (*impatiently*). Oh yes! Columbus is a great man—a very great man now, to be sure! One hears his name gabbled everywhere: "Columbus! Columbus! Columbus!" The very sound of it is like the galloping of a donkey!

3RD GENTLEMAN. Also, when he comes into the room, men rise from their seats as if he were Royalty.

2ND GENTLEMAN. And now, the more to prove his importance, he allows himself to be late. [*Outside a clock is heard striking the hour.*]

4TH GENTLEMAN. Not late, Señor. The hour is now striking.

[COLUMBUS *enters, and bows to the company. Attendants go to take from him his hat, cloak and sword.*]

COLUMBUS. Good-evening, Señors. I hope I have not kept you waiting?

2ND GENTLEMAN (*mockingly*). On the contrary, Admiral, you are most punctual. As punctual as a King.

COLUMBUS. But not so punctual as my appetite, Señor. I had that an hour ago.

1ST GENTLEMAN. Then let us sit down.

[*They seat themselves.* COLUMBUS *is given the place of honour. The servers go round and wait upon the company with meat and wine.*]

3RD GENTLEMAN. Señor Columbus, when do you return to your kingdom ?

COLUMBUS. My kingdom ?

3RD GENTLEMAN. The land you discovered, Señor.

COLUMBUS. I do not know, Señor. When the Queen sends me I shall go—not before.

2ND GENTLEMAN. And do you expect any difficulty ? On the voyage, I mean.

COLUMBUS. Only the usual difficulties, Señor, of wind and weather.

2ND GENTLEMAN. In fact, Señor, no more difficulty than you had the *first* time ?

COLUMBUS (*smiling*). Certainly no *more*, Señor.

3RD GENTLEMAN. You are very fortunate, Admiral.

COLUMBUS. In what way, Señor ?

3RD GENTLEMAN. That having encountered those " usual difficulties " you have now become such a great man.

COLUMBUS. The difficulties, the first time, Señor were *not* usual.

2ND GENTLEMAN. Indeed ? Wind and weather, you said. What else was there to hinder you ?

COLUMBUS. The Unknown, Señor; and men's fear of it.

2ND GENTLEMAN. On the contrary, Señor; men *love* the Unknown. They search for it. They live for it. They die for it.

COLUMBUS (*gravely*). Many have died for it: yes. Some of my own comrades did so.

3RD GENTLEMAN. Quite so. Some died that you might live and become " great." Again I say, you were fortunate.

COLUMBUS. What exactly do you mean, Señor, by " fortunate "?

3RD GENTLEMAN. I mean, Señor Columbus, that had you not made the discovery just when you did, I, or somebody else, might quite easily have made it for ourselves a year later. In fact, I was intending to !

[*At this there is some laughter from the company.*]

COLUMBUS. " Quite easily " ? Had you then, also, found a way ?

3RD GENTLEMAN. The way was there, Señor. You had but to sail west far enough to find the East waiting for you. Nobody could have missed it.

COLUMBUS. For everything that can possibly be done, Señor, the way is always there. The thing is—to find it. For instance——
[*He pauses.*]

2ND GENTLEMAN. " For instance " ?   Yes ?

COLUMBUS (*mockingly*). Do you know, Señor, the way to make an egg stand on end ?

2ND GENTLEMAN. Really, I have never tried.

3RD GENTLEMAN. Make an egg stand on end ? Impossible !

COLUMBUS. Oh no, Señor; not if you know the *way*.

1ST GENTLEMAN. An amusing game ! We will send for one, and try.
[*He makes a sign to one of the servers, who goes, and presently returns, bringing an egg with him.   Meanwhile the talk goes on.*]

5TH GENTLEMAN. Señor Columbus, do you think that *you* can do it ?

COLUMBUS. I know that I can do it, Señor.

2ND GENTLEMAN. What if you fail?

COLUMBUS. Then I will admit that, in making my discovery, also, I have done nothing worth telling about. But, if I succeed, Señor? . . .

3RD GENTLEMAN. If you make an egg stand on its end, while I count ten, then I will give you a hundred doubloons to help you to your next discovery.

COLUMBUS. I thank you, Señor. That will be very acceptable.

1ST GENTLEMAN. Ah! Here is the egg.

COLUMBUS. Which of you will begin, Señors?

2ND GENTLEMAN. You. It is *you* who say you can do it.

COLUMBUS. Ah! But I am only the son of a cloth-weaver. Gentlemen of noble birth should go first. . . . Are you afraid, Señor, to " show me the way " ?

[*The* 2ND GENTLEMAN *takes up the egg, and tries. The others watch him, and laugh.*]

2ND GENTLEMAN (*giving it up*). Psha! Impossible!

COLUMBUS. But try again—differently.

2ND GENTLEMAN. How—" differently " ?

COLUMBUS. Try the other end.

2ND GENTLEMAN (*having tried*). I have tried both ends. It is impossible.

COLUMBUS (*to* 3RD GENTLEMAN). Will *you* try, Señor ?

3RD GENTLEMAN. I will not make a fool of myself; for I see it is impossible.

COLUMBUS (*to* 1ST GENTLEMAN). You, Señor ?

1ST GENTLEMAN (*laughing*). I would rather see someone else do it.

2ND GENTLEMAN. Well, Señor Columbus—now you. Do *you* think you can do it ?

COLUMBUS. God helping me, and with a little common sense, nothing is easier—if only one does it *the right way.* . . . There !
[*He brings the egg smartly down on the table, breaking the end of it.   The egg stands.*]

COLUMBUS (*to* 3RD GENTLEMAN). Count ten, Señor !

2ND GENTLEMAN (*and others*). That is a trick ! A trick !

COLUMBUS. Why, yes! Call it a trick if you like; and I have won it. A hundred doubloons, please, Señor. (*To* 2ND GENTLE-MAN) The *way* is easy enough, when you have been shown it. It only needs a firm hand, Señors. The question was, who should be master—you, or the egg? The egg mastered you; but I mastered the egg. And that is what I did when I made my first voyage. I mastered an egg which had never before been broken. That egg was the Unknown.

4TH GENTLEMAN. He is right! He is right, Señors!

COLUMBUS. That was " the way." Now that you *know* the way, it seems easy.

2ND GENTLEMAN (*as he hands over the doubloons*). Well, well, Señor Columbus, I will argue with you no further.

COLUMBUS. You had better not, Señor.

1ST GENTLEMAN. Gentlemen, let us drink to the health of Columbus, who has now proved to us that if you can master an egg, you can master anything!
[*They drink, with laughter.*]

TWO MARTYRS

Reign of Henry VIII, 1509-1547

WITHIN two years of each other, two great and good Englishmen died for their faith, though in their faith they differed. How did this come about ?

In Western Europe, during the thousand years of the Middle Ages, men and women were all members of one Church, with the Pope at Rome as its head.

Then in the sixteenth century, during the years of the Tudors, came the great change. For a time there was fierce division among Christians. Some became Reformers, or Protestants. Others remained Roman Catholics, loyal to the Pope. And in those days men and women felt so deeply about their faith that they were ready to die for it, and to make others die who differed from them. Ever since that time—about 400 years ago— there have been different kinds of Christians in England as elsewhere.

On each side, during the great change,

there were good and great men who died for their faith. Sir Thomas More was one of those who held to the old form of faith and died for it. On the other side was William Tyndale, who joined the Reformers, and died for his faith also.

William Tyndale, the Reformer, was born in the reign of the first Tudor King, Henry VII, and he died in the reign of the second Tudor King, Henry VIII. He was born on the borders of Wales; he studied both at Oxford and at Cambridge; and when quite young he became a priest.

His first great work was the translation of the Bible into English, and his Bible is the basis of the English Bible we read today. The thought of translating the Bible came to him quite early. He said of himself that he " began to smell the Word of God " while still a student at Cambridge. Soon after, having decided to start the work, he told a priest whom he found ignorant of the Scriptures: " If God spare my life, ere many years I will cause a boy that driveth the plough shall know more of the Scriptures than thou dost."

Saying that sort of thing did not make

him popular with his brother clergy, and he found it wiser to give up his country living and go to London.

There he stayed for some months in the house of a friend, working hard at his translation of the New Testament. But finding that it would be impossible to publish it in England—because in those days it was against the law—he went over to Germany; and going for greater safety from place to place, he finished the work and got it printed.

Having done that, the next thing was to get it smuggled into England; and at last copies of his New Testament came over hidden in bales of Flemish cloth, and numbers of them went secretly from hand to hand throughout the country.

A merchant, who was a friend of Tyndale, brought word to the Archbishop of Canterbury that more of Tyndale's Bibles were waiting to be brought over to England; and the Archbishop was so anxious to destroy them that he paid a good price for them, and had every copy burned.

When Tyndale heard what the merchant had done, he was quite pleased. The money, he said, would pay his debts, and enable

The Gospell off Sancte Jhon.

The fyrst Chapter.

IN the begynnynge was that worde/ãd that worde was with god: and god was thatt worde. The same was in the begynnynge wyth god. All thyngf were made by it/ and with out it/ was made noo thige/ that made was. In it was lyfe/ And lyfe was the light of men/ And the light shyneth i darcknes/ ãd darcknes cõprehëded it not.

There was a mã sent from god/ whose name was Jhon. The same cã as a witnes/ to beare witnes of the light/ that all men through hi myght beleve. He was nott that light: but to beare witnes of the light. That was a true light/ which lighteneth all men that come ito the worlde. He was in the worlde/ ãd the worlde by hi was made: and the worlde knewe hym not.

He cã ito his awne/ ãd his receaved hi not. vnto as meny as receaved hi/ gave he power to be the sõnes of god: i that they beleved õ his name: which were borne not of bloude nor of the will of the flesshe/ nor yet of the will of men: but of god. And that worde was made flesshe/ and dwelt amonge vs/ and we sawe the glory off yt/ as the glory off the only begotten sonne off the father.

THE FIRST FOURTEEN VERSES OF CHAPTER I OF TYNDALE'S TRANSLATION OF THE GOSPEL OF ST. JOHN.

Compare it with the Translation of the Authorised Version

him to print a new and better edition; while
the burning of God's Word would make the
world cry out against the Archbishop, and so
do good to the cause of the Reformers.

But now, having done so great a work, and
with more still to do, he was a marked man;
and wherever he went were enemies plotting
to deprive him of life or freedom. The last
five years of his life were spent in Antwerp,
where he worked and was seen only by his
friends, hardly ever going out for fear of
arrest.

Then one day there came to him a man
who pretended to be his friend; he asked
Tyndale for help, and borrowed money of
him. And having thus got his confidence,
one day he lured Tyndale to the door of the
house in which he had found safe shelter;
and there at the door men were waiting
secretly, who at once laid hands on Tyndale
and carried him off to prison and to death.
" If they shall burn me," he had said some
years earlier, " they shall do none other
thing than I have looked for. There is none
other way of entering into the Kingdom of
Heaven than through suffering of pain and
of very death after the example of Christ."

THIS IS A PORTRAIT OF SIR THOMAS MORE, DRAWN BY ONE OF
THE BEST PORTRAIT PAINTERS IN THE WORLD, HANS
HOLBEIN, WHO STAYED WITH MORE FOR THREE YEARS.

More was of middle height, had a pale complexion, black hair,
and grey eyes with dark spots. His expression in this
picture is serious, but a great friend said of him, " He has
the quickest sense of the ridiculous of anyone I ever met."

Thus, William Tyndale, the Reformer, suffered death for his faith.

So also did the other great and good man, Sir Thomas More, who remained true to the Roman Church.

Sir Thomas More was " the most delightful man in England." " All the birds in Chelsea," where he lived, " come to him to be fed," wrote a friend; " and he has various tame animals—a monkey, a fox, a ferret, and a weasel. . . . He has never made an enemy nor become an enemy. His whole house breathes happiness, and no one enters it who is not the better for the visit."

For some time Sir Thomas More was in the King's favour. Henry VIII would go down to his house at Chelsea and dine with him, and afterwards would walk with him in his garden, his arm about More's neck, a mark of affection which the King showed to no other of his subjects. To his son-in-law, who congratulated him on so great a sign of the royal favour, More answered: " I find his grace my very good lord, indeed; and I believe he favours me as much as any subject within this realm; but if my head would win him a castle in France, off it would go."

And a few years later, off his head indeed did go, but for another reason. After Henry VIII had broken with the Pope, Sir Thomas More refused to take an oath denying the Pope's authority; and for that, on a charge of treason, he was sent to the scaffold.

At the foot of the scaffold, finding that the steps up to it were shaky, he said to the constable who had charge of him: " See me safe up ! I can shift for myself as I come down." And just as he had laid down his head upon the block, he lifted it again, and carefully moved his beard to one side, saying: " Pity to cut that which has not committed treason."

And so, with a brave joke on his lips, he died—one of England's wisest men.

THE TRAGEDY OF A QUEEN

Reign of Elizabeth, 1558-1603

THERE was a time, in our Tudor period, when two famous Queens were living in England at the same time. One of these was the daughter of Henry VIII, Queen Elizabeth : great, successful, powerful, loved and admired by her people, she ruled wisely and well, and made England a strong nation.

The other was Mary Stuart, Queen of Scotland : very beautiful and very unfortunate. Driven out of her own country, she had fled to England for safety; and in England she was kept a prisoner till the day of her death, nineteen years later.

The story of Mary Stuart is one of the saddest and most famous in history. When she was only a few days old, her father died, and she became Queen of Scotland. When five years old she was taken to France; at sixteen she married the heir to the French throne, and for six months she was the

Queen of France. But two years after her marriage her husband died, and then she returned to Scotland.

The Scottish people did not love her; many of them had become Reformers, whereas she was a Roman Catholic. Jealous and suspicious, they looked on her as a foreigner and a stranger. She made an unhappy marriage with her cousin, Lord Darnley; and when, a few years later, he was found murdered, many suspected that Mary herself had agreed to his death.

Soon after, she took as her third husband the man who was known to have plotted Darnley's death. Some say that she loved him, some that he married her by force. Led by some of the nobles, her people then rose in rebellion, and having defeated her in battle, they imprisoned her in Lochleven Castle, which stood on an island in a lake.

From this castle she escaped by the help of a page. The governor used to keep all the house keys beside him on his table at supper. One evening, when dusk was coming on, and it was getting dark in the hall, the page dropped a napkin over the keys and swept them off the table without making any

THE STATE ENTRY OF MARY STUART INTO EDINBURGH
AFTER HER RETURN FROM FRANCE.

She was successful at first in winning over many of her subjects.

noise. That night, when everyone had gone to bed, the page led the Queen and her waiting-woman down to a boat which lay ready outside the walls; and having put a light in a window as a signal to his friends who were waiting on the further shore, he locked the gates so that no one could follow, and rowed the Queen safely across the lake, dropping the keys into the water on the way.

But though Mary thus made her escape, her freedom did not last long. Within two weeks the army which had been raised to restore her to the throne was utterly defeated by the rebel lords; and Mary, seeing that no hope remained, rode sixty miles without stopping from Scotland into England, and then thirty miles more to Carlisle, all in the same day.

In going to England she made a great mistake. Had she been able to go to France she would have been safe. But in England many people who were Catholics regarded her as the true heir to the throne, and would have been glad to see Elizabeth killed or dethroned, and Mary put in her place. So the English Queen and her ministers, who feared for Elizabeth's safety, caused Mary to be kept a prisoner.

At first Mary was treated well, and though always under guard, she was allowed a good deal of freedom. But when plots were dis-covered—not only for her escape, but against the life of Queen Elizabeth herself—she was moved to a place of greater safety, and her imprisonment became more severe.

For nineteen years this beautiful and un-happy woman, who had been a reigning Queen, first of France and then of Scotland, was kept in England, a prisoner. It must have been very dull for her at times. We have a letter she wrote, asking for some pretty little dogs to be sent her in baskets, very warmly packed. "For besides reading and work-ing," she says, "I take pleasure only in the little animals I can get."

Later on, she was charged with conspiring against the Queen's life and the safety of the realm, and she was beheaded in the great Hall of Fotheringay Castle. Her faithful little dog had crept to the scaffold unnoticed, and would not leave its mistress even when she was dead.

The year following the beheading of Mary

Stuart, came the Spanish Armada.   Had that succeeded and Mary been still alive, there can be little doubt that Elizabeth would have been dethroned, and Mary Stuart made Queen of England in her place.

MARY QUEEN OF SCOTS DESCENDING THE STAIRCASE ON THE WAY TO THE HALL WHERE SHE WAS EXECUTED.

Her head-dress was of lawn with a long flowing white veil.

SAILING ROUND THE WORLD

1577-1580

N April 4th, 1581, Queen Elizabeth made a journey to Deptford, and there, on the deck of the first English ship that had gone round the world, she knighted the first man of any nation who had commanded throughout such a voyage.

A DUTCH PORTRAIT OF DRAKE OF ABOUT THE YEAR 1581.

The man was Francis Drake, and this is his story.

The discovery of America by Columbus had doubled the size of the world to the travellers who came after him. Far away in the West, they heard, was a great continent full of rich treasures—gold, and silver, and spices.

The Spaniards had got there first; and because they discovered it, they tried to prevent other nations from having a share in the richest part of it, wishing to keep its trade and riches to themselves. So when

328

English trading ships came into those parts, they attacked and drove them away, or even destroyed them.

They did this, on one occasion, to some ships under the command of a seaman called Sir John Hawkins, who had gone out to trade in the Gulf of Mexico. Two of the five ships escaped; and the captain of one of these was a young seaman named Francis Drake.

Drake had put all his money into the venture; and now it was lost. He tried to get it back from the Spaniards, but they would not listen to him; so he made up his mind to get it back in his own way.

With only two ships under his command, he sailed to the West Indies, and having discovered the Spanish trade routes, the harbours to which their ships came, and the towns in which their treasure lay stored, he returned home, and the next year started to carry out his plan for paying himself back. Going from island to island, he captured what Spanish ships he could find and robbed them of their treasure. He even attacked a town on the mainland, and carried off from the governor's house as much silver as his boats could load.

Then he landed on the Isthmus of Panama, where the distance from sea to sea is less than fifty miles. And one day, led by a native guide, he climbed a hill; and on top of the hill he climbed a tree; and there, looking east and west, he saw both oceans— the Atlantic and the Pacific—those two great bodies of water which divided the New World from the Old.

It was the first time Drake had seen the Pacific, though he had already heard of it; and being a man of adventure and a great sailor, he could not see it without wishing to sail on it. So there, up in the tree, he " prayed God of His goodness to give him life and leave to sail once in an English ship in that sea."

Drake returned home from this voyage a rich man. He was a townsman of Plymouth; and there the fame of his adventures had already given him a great name. He arrived on a Sunday morning; most of the people were in church: it was sermon time.

Into the church came word that Drake's ships were back in harbour. The church emptied itself; no one waited for the sermon

THE " GOLDEN HIND " AT ANCHOR.
A Dutch picture drawn some ten years after Drake's voyage.
The *Golden Hind* was a fast sailing ship of 150 tons.

to finish. All wanted to greet their great townsman on his return, and to hear his news.

In 1577 Drake started on his greatest voyage of all—his voyage round the world. It was because of his having climbed that tree that Drake was the first man to sail an English ship round the world. Fifty years before, a ship commanded by a Portuguese, named Magellan, had made that great voyage; but Magellan died on the way.

Drake was to have better fortune—not only to do it, but to live for many years after.

When Drake first set out on this voyage, he did not mean to go further than the other side of America, and then back again. It was still only the plunder of Spanish ships and towns that he intended. For this reason, so that the Spaniards should not hear of it, he made a secret of where he was going; even the men of his ships' crews did not know.

He set out with three ships, and sailed, not to the West Indies as before, but south-west to the coast of Brazil. Then, following the coast southward, he entered the Straits of Magellan; and having reached that point, in honour of the event, he re-named his ship the *Golden Hind*.

Then followed disaster; for fifty-two days storm raged; one of his three ships was sunk, another turned and went home again. The *Golden Hind* went on alone.

For more than a year Drake and his men sailed from place to place along the western coast of America, from south to north. He had with him only about a hundred men; but coming unexpectedly upon the Spanish trading stations, he captured ships and towns and treasure, until his own vessel was as full as it would hold of the gold and silver and jewels which the Spaniards had meant to carry back with them to Europe.

The Spaniards soon found that this Englishman, who was paying himself back so largely for the damage they had done him in former years, was no ordinary man. A Spanish gentleman who met him during this voyage wrote the following account of him: " A man thirty-five years old, of small size with a reddish beard; and one of the greatest sailors that exist, both from his skill and his power of command. He has a hundred men, all in the prime of life, and as well trained for war as if they were old soldiers of Italy. Each one is specially careful to keep his weapons clean. He treats them with affection and they treat him with respect. . . . He dines and sups to the music of violins."

From this same account we learn that Drake loved perfumes, and silver plate and fine clothes; that even in his life of hard adventures and danger he lived like a fine gentleman, and had beautiful things around him.

Drake's voyage had now lasted for two years; he had got as much booty as he could carry; it was time to return home. But Drake knew that if he went back the way he had come the Spaniards would lie in wait for him with a strong force to take back what they had lost. So first he sailed north, hoping to find a way over the Polar Sea along the northern coast of America. But as he went north it grew colder and colder, and the winds blew contrary; so at last he turned and sailed south and west, crossed the Pacific, and passing through the islands lying to the south of Asia, came at last to the coast of Africa.

At every place where he landed he added to the riches of his cargo. Never was a ship, on a single voyage, so richly and variously laden from so many lands: gold and silver, pearls and precious stones, silks and spices— with all these his ship was stuffed as full as it would hold.

But when he rounded the Cape of Good Hope, eight months after leaving America, he had only fifty-seven men left, and three casks of water. From the Cape to England took another four months. He landed in

GILOLO IN.

Tarenate   Tidor: Mutir   Machian   Bachian

Quam mirifice a Rege Moluccarum tubaru clangorem admirantz, intrƷvectus fuerit, delineatio.

THE "GOLDEN HIND" IN THE SPICE ISLANDS BEING TOWED INTO HARBOUR, TO THE SOUND OF THE TRUMPETS, BY WAR-CANOES BELONGING TO THE SULTAN OF TERNATE.

A small picture drawn by a Dutchman some ten years after Drake's voyage.

Plymouth on November 3rd, 1580, having been away for nearly three years.

His fame went through all England. Queen Elizabeth sent for him; and when he had brought his ship to Deptford on the Thames, she went on board and dined with him; and then, as a mark of her approval of all that he had done, she conferred on him the honour of knighthood. And so he became *Sir* Francis Drake.

Seven years later, with only four ships, he entered the harbour of Cadiz, and burned part of the Spanish fleet, which was then preparing for an invasion of England. " I have singed the King of Spain's beard," was his own account of the matter when he returned from that exploit.

The next year, in 1588, he fought as Captain on one of the English ships which broke and defeated the Spanish Armada. The story is told that when word came to Plymouth that the Armada had been sighted at the mouth of the Channel, Drake, with other captains, was playing a game of bowls. " There is plenty of time," said Drake, " to finish the game, and beat the Spaniards too."

So the game was finished; and that being done, off went Drake with the rest to beat the Spaniards.

KINGS AND QUEENS IN TUDOR
AND STUART TIMES

TODAY it is only on great public occasions — such as when the Monarch comes to open Parliament—that the old forms of state are still observed. But 400 years ago, in Tudor times, the Monarch was surrounded with ceremony every day. Men who lived in those days have left us an account of what those ceremonies were like. And this is the way that Queen Elizabeth kept state every Sunday in her palace at Greenwich on the Thames.

When church time drew near, all her Court stood gathered waiting for her: the Archbishop of Canterbury and the Bishop of London, Lords, Ladies, Councillors of State, Officers of the Crown and Gentlemen of the Court. Then a door opened and out came the Queen, led and followed by lords and attendants. First came Gentlemen, then Barons, then Earls, then Knights of the Garter. After them followed the Lord Chancellor bearing his seals of office, walking between two noblemen, one of whom carried the royal sceptre, the other the sword of state in a red scabbard.

Then, walking alone, came the Queen splendidly attired, her dress covered with pearls, a crown upon her head, and her long train borne behind her by a great Court lady. Wherever she turned her face as she passed, people went down upon their knees, and remained kneeling while she spoke to them. In the ante-chapel were others waiting to present petitions, and as she took them the people shouted, "God save Queen Elizabeth!" and the Queen answered, "I thank you, my good people." That is the way a Queen went to church 350 years ago.

And while the service was going on, the royal table was being laid for dinner, with as much ceremony as though the Queen were already present. First came a gentleman bearing a rod, and behind him another with a tablecloth; and having knelt down three times they laid the cloth upon the table. Then, having knelt once more, they retired, and in their places came two others carrying a salt cellar and a plate with bread on it.

QUEEN ELIZABETH AT A HUNTING PICNIC.

Notice the costumes, and the amount of food and the pages !

And these two having knelt in like manner three times, placed what they had brought on the table and retired also.

Then came two ladies, one carrying a carving-knife, while the other, after kneeling as all the others had done, took bread and salt and rubbed the plates with it so as to make them quite clean for the Queen to eat from. Then came thirty-four yeomen of the guard in scarlet uniforms, carrying the courses of meat, twenty-four dishes to each course. And the lady with the carving-knife cut off a piece of meat from each dish and gave it to the man who carried it, and the man had to eat it so as to make sure that the meat was not poisoned. Thus was the Queen's dinner made ready for her. And all the time this was going on twelve trumpets and two kettle-drums were being sounded, making the hall ring with their noise.

Yet after so much ceremony had taken place, the Queen did not sit down to that table at all, but going through into an inner chamber, took her meal alone; and what she did not eat of the twenty-four dishes of each course the ladies and gentlemen of her Court,

Touching for the " King's Evil."

sitting down at the larger table, were allowed
to have for themselves.

It seems to us a very troublesome way of
dining, and one wonders how, with so much
ceremony in the day, Kings and Queens
were able to get through all that they had
to do. But that is how, in former times,
Kings and Queens were expected to live, so
that people might be constantly reminded of
the dignity of their rank, and the sacredness
of their persons.

Another ceremony expected of our Kings
in those days was the touching for " the
King's evil."

The ceremony arose from an old belief
that the King was so sacred a person that
his touch could heal certain diseases. And
so, on appointed days and times, people
suffering from sickness were brought to him
to be touched and healed. An eyewitness,
in the reign of James I, has left an account
of how this ceremony was performed. After
the King had been to church, when the
service was over, his chair was moved to a
table, and there he seated himself. Then
the King's physician, having first examined
them to see if they were truly suffering from

sickness, brought to him first a little girl, then two boys, then a tall youth. Each in turn was made to kneel down before the King; and because the chief disease which the King was supposed to heal shows itself in the neck, the King reached out his finger and touched the neck of each one in turn; and as he did so he said—but speaking in French—" The King touches: may God heal you !"

Then taking up a piece of money—one for each person—he hung it by a white ribbon round the neck of each, and while all this was going on, a Bishop stood by his side and read prayers, and a chaplain knelt before him to make the responses and say " Amen."

When the ceremony was over three lords came with water in a golden jug, and a golden basin and a towel; and the King washed his hand very carefully, so that he might not himself catch the disease which he was trying to cure.

We are told that King James very much disliked having to perform this ceremony. But Charles II touched nearly 100,000 people in the course of his reign.

For nearly a hundred years after the reign of James I, the ceremony still went on; and one of the last times that we hear about it was when a small child was brought to be touched by Queen Anne. That small child grew up to be a very famous man, Dr. Samuel Johnson. But we are not told that the Queen's touch cured him.

THE PILGRIM FATHERS

1620

ON a cold November day in the year 1620, some hundred persons landed from a small ship on the sandy shores behind Cape Cod in North America.

This happened in the reign of James I, the son of Queen Mary Stuart, and the successor to Queen Elizabeth. He was the first of our Stuart Kings.

The story of the Two Martyrs shows how strongly men and women in those times felt about their faith. And these travellers who landed in North America had gone from England to make a new home for themselves where they might worship God in their own way.

Some of them had been to Holland, but finding it hard to make a decent living in a foreign land, they came back to England, and starting from Plymouth in a small ship, with all their families, they set out for the New World.

HERE IS AN OLD PICTURE OF AN INDIAN VILLAGE IN NORTH
AMERICA.

Notice the stockade round the Village, and the Temple
(marked A), and the Chief's house (marked B), and the
pond whence water was obtained (marked C).

Their ship was named the *Mayflower*, and those who went in it became known as the " Pilgrim Fathers."

The Pilgrim Fathers went to make a New England in a new country 3,000 miles away; and so doing this they became the first founders of the great American nation; for after them went others—many hundreds— taking their household goods and their farm implements with them. And so within the next generation the new Colony was well started, and had begun to prosper.

But it was the Pilgrim Fathers who, by years of hard labour and harder suffering, prepared the way. Landing at a port which earlier settlers had, curiously enough, called Plymouth, they started to build and dig and plough, in land which was then all wilderness. In the long and bitterly cold winter which followed, half of them died, through sickness and famine, but the rest toiled on. For a time they never knew at night where they would get food the next day. But through hardship and discontent they held on; and, even in their days of great difficulty, others came out and joined them.

Happily the Pilgrim Fathers were friendly

with the native Red Indians from the outset. One of the leading settlers knew medicine; he saved the life of an Indian chief, and the Indians were so grateful that they befriended the settlers, and taught them how to grow maize.

" Let it not be grievous to you," wrote friends at home, hearing of their troubles, " that you have been able to break the ice for others. The honour shall be yours to the world's end."

That prophecy still holds good. The " Pilgrim Fathers " and the *Mayflower* are names which will ever be remembered in our history and in the history of America.

" I shall call that my country," said one of the Pilgrim Fathers, " where I may most glorify God, and enjoy the presence of my dearest friends."

THE KING AND THE COMMONS

AT two o'clock in the afternoon of January 30th, 1649, a King stepped out of a window of the Banqueting House, which still stands at Whitehall. He stepped out on to a scaffold—to meet his death at the hands of an executioner.

How did this tragedy come about ? It arose out of quarrels between the King and the Parliament. They differed on questions of religion; and they differed on questions of power, the King wanting to keep his power, while the Parliament wanted to extend theirs.

The quarrel grew hot. Some of the leaders of the Parliament were charged by the King with conspiring and rebelling against him, and the King wanted to have them arrested. So he sent to the House of Commons, claiming that five of them should be handed over to justice.

Much to the King's annoyance the Com-

349

PORTRAIT OF CHARLES I.
This is an engraving after a portrait by Van Dyck, Charles I's
favourite painter.

mons did not at once obey and the five members were not ordered into custody. So the next day, while the House of Commons was sitting, the King went down to Westminster with an armed body of two hundred men. Then he stepped through the door into the House of Commons—the first King who had ever done so. He walked up to the Speaker, and said, " By your leave, Mr. Speaker, I must borrow your chair a little."

Then the King, looking round the House, saw that the five members he had come to arrest were not there—for they had been warned of the King's approach. The King then made a short speech. " Gentlemen," he said, " I am sorry for this occasion of coming unto you. Yesterday I sent a sergeant-at-arms to apprehend some that by my command were accused of high treason; whereunto I did expect obedience." He then asked whether the five members were there; and when no one answered him, he turned to the Speaker and repeated the question.

The Speaker, in all humility, went down upon his knees; but his answer was brave. It was his duty, he said, to have neither eyes

CHARLES I AT THE GUILDHALL, 1642.

Charles went there to demand the five members who had taken
refuge in the City. But the Lord Mayor and Common
Council of the City refused to give them up, and the King
left to the shouts of " Privileges of Parliament." In this
picture the King, followed by some of his courtiers, is being
received by the Lord Mayor.

nor tongue, to see or say anything save what the House commanded him.

"Well, well," replied the King, "'tis no matter. My eyes are as good as another's."

There was a long pause; everyone stood silent, while the King looked carefully to right and left of him for the missing members. "I see," he said at last, "the birds have flown; but I expect you to send them to me."

No one answered. There was nothing more to be done. Having failed in his attempt, the King had to go back empty-handed. As he left, behind his back came angry cries of "Privilege! Privilege!" For had the five members been there, all knew that the armed men, waiting outside at the King's command, would have carried them away by force. "I warrant you," said one of the King's followers, raising his pistol, "I am a good marksman; I will hit sure."

All through the City of London went word of what the King had done. When next day he went to demand from the Lord Mayor the arrest of the five members wherever they might be found, he was followed through

THE BANQUETING HOUSE AT WHITEHALL.
Charles I stepped out on to the scaffold from the middle window.

the streets by cries from the citizens, protesting against his treating Parliament in this way.

After that there was no mending the quarrel. The five members came back to the House, defended from arrest by a strong band of armed citizens. The city became so hostile that Charles and his Court were forced to leave London.

Seven years of civil war followed.

When Charles next returned to London he

came as a prisoner. And those who were then in power had him tried and executed on a charge of high treason against the rights and liberties of the people of England. This was in the year 1649.

Charles I met his end bravely. It was a bitterly cold day, and Charles put on an extra shirt, which can still be seen at Windsor Castle. " Let me have a shirt on more than ordinary, by reason the season is so sharp as probably may make me shake, which some observers may imagine proceeds from fear. . . . I fear not death. Death is not terrible to me : I bless my God I am prepared."

Of the brave way in which Charles I faced death upon the scaffold at Whitehall, a poet living at the time wrote these lines :

" He nothing common did or mean
   Upon that memorable scene,
      But with his keener eye
      The axe's edge did try ;
   Nor called the gods, with vulgar spite,
   To vindicate his helpless right ;
      But bowed his comely head
      Down as upon a bed."

THE PILGRIM WHO WENT TO PRISON

AFTER the execution of Charles I England had no King for eleven years. During most of this time the great Puritan, Oliver Cromwell, ruled the country. Then, on his death, Charles's eldest son was restored to the throne as Charles II.

It was during Charles II's reign that the famous book called *The Pilgrim's Progress* was written. It reads like a fairy story, but it tells of a Christian's life. And the man, John Bunyan, who wrote it, wrote it in prison.

He was the son of a tinker who had a forge and workshop. He learned to read and write at the village school; but afterwards—from never reading—he forgot, and his wife had to teach him again. In his childhood he worked at his father's trade.

When he was seventeen, he became a soldier on the side of the Parliament, in the Civil War against the King.

As a boy he was very fond of playing hockey and tip-cat;[1] as a youth he loved dancing; and he was also a bell-ringer. But in those days many good men, called Puritans, thought that such things were wrong: and Bunyan, thinking as they did, feared that his love of games was a sin; and he often tried to break himself of the habit, but could not.

One day when he was playing tip-cat, he had just made a stroke with the stick when he thought he heard a voice calling him from Heaven to leave all such things and live a new life for the service of God only. For some years he held back; and though he led a sober and industrious life, and when he married cared well for his wife and children, he thought himself a great sinner. He himself tells the story how once, in deep misery of mind, he sat down on a stone in the street, and felt himself cut off from all the life around him.

Then he was converted and became a preacher; and he preached so well that all

[1] A game in which the wooden cat, or tip-cat, is struck at one end so as to spring up, and then knocked a distance by the same player.

round Bedford, where he lived, he became famous.

But, in the reign of Charles II, people were not allowed to preach unless they had a licence; and if they preached without leave, or in places other than the churches of the land, they were sent to prison. And Bunyan, like many others, refused to be bound by a law which was against his conscience. So he was sent to Bedford Gaol. There he remained, on and off, for nearly twelve years. " If you let me out today, I will preach again tomorrow," he said.

It was during that time in prison that he wrote his great book, *The Pilgrim's Progress*. Perhaps if he had not been sent to prison he would never have found the time to write it. But because he had a glad heart and a strong will, he did the great thing of his life while he was a prisoner.

In that book you read the story of a man named " Christian," who had a heavy bundle on his back—a dark bundle of sin—and of how he tried to get rid of it; and how, going on a long journey to find the city of God, he had many adventures by the way. He met evil men who robbed and imprisoned him, and others who mocked or deceived him. He met giants, and demons, and savage beasts. Sometimes he had to go by dark ways full of dangers, and swim through deep waters. But in spite of all these difficulties he got safely through, and saw the city open its gates to him with a sound of music and shouting. And in the second half of the story we read how his wife and children followed him, and came to the same good end.

BUNYAN DREAMING THE STORY OF THE PILGRIM'S PROGRESS.

Notice " Christian," with the load on his back, leaving the City of Destruction for the City of God.

All the time Bunyan wrote his book, he also made long-tagged laces and sold them to the hawkers for the support of his family. And his wife and children used to come and see him, and cheer him in his prison; and, of all these, the one he loved most tenderly was a little daughter who had been born blind.

In the prison he would still preach, though it was the thing he had been forbidden to do. For the prison was full of many others like himself, who had been sent there for the same reason; and though the law might stop them from preaching outside, it could not stop them in prison.

So Bunyan finished his book in Bedford Gaol: and after twelve years he was let out again. Then his book was printed and published, and at once it became famous.

When riding to London from Reading in heavy rain he caught a severe cold and died from it. But before he died many copies of his book had been printed and had been read by thousands. People have gone on reading it ever since: for it is one of the greatest books that has ever been written in this country.

THE SONG OF THE PILGRIM

HE who would valiant be
  'Gainst all disaster,
Let him in constancy
  Follow the Master.
There's no discouragement
Shall make him once relent
His first avowed intent
  To be a Pilgrim.

Who-so beset him round
  With dismal stories,
Do but themselves confound;
  His strength the more is.
No foes shall stay his might;
Though he with giants fight,
He will make good his right
  To be a Pilgrim.

Since, Lord, Thou dost defend
  Us with Thy Spirit,
We know we, at the end,
  Shall life inherit.
Then, fancies flee away!
I'll fear not what men say;
I'll labour night and day
  To be a Pilgrim.

JOHN BUNYAN.

THE FIRE OF LONDON

LONDON is now the largest city in the world; and in the course of its long history many famous things have happened to it. Of these two of the biggest and worst events were the Plague and the Great Fire, which took place 270 years ago in the reign of Charles II.

First came the Plague, a disease of which in a single year many thousands died. The same sort of thing had happened before, but never on so large a scale; and the reason was that in those days houses had no drains, and people threw their refuse into the streets, and drank foul water. London had grown great, but London had not learned how to keep itself clean.

And then, the next year, came the Great Fire, and Old London was burned up. The narrow streets and the half-timbered houses gave the flames everything they wanted; there was no stopping them.

The Fire lasted for four whole days—leap-

CHEAPSIDE IN THE SIXTEENTH CENTURY.

To the left is a building of stone from which Royal persons used
to watch pageants and processions. On the left also is
Goldsmith's Row, a timber building, four stories high, with
ten gables. In the background of the picture is old St.
Paul's (on the left with the spire).

ing from house to house and from street to
street, faster than a man could run. In that
great Fire old St. Paul's Cathedral was
burned, and with it 87 churches, many
famous streets, including Cheapside, and
more than 13,000 houses. It was one of
the greatest fires that has ever been known.

And so the old City of London was destroyed in Charles II's reign, and a new
city with a new St. Paul's and new churches
had to be built. This time most of the
streets were made wider, and were built of
brick or stone only; and many other im-
provements were made. And on all sides
the city grew and grew, made rich by its
trade.

London goes on growing still; and now
its streets are not nearly wide enough
for all the traffic that has to go through
them; and they are so dangerous to cross,
that almost as many people get killed in a
single year, as were killed by the Plague in
the year 1665.

THE FIRE OF LONDON.

Notice on further side of river on extreme right the Tower of London, and on left centre old St. Paul's, which is burning. Notice also London Bridge with the houses on it, and on the nearer side of river, Southwark Cathedral.

LONDON'S BURNING!

LONDON town is burning down !
   None knows whose doing.
Hark, how all the fire-bells call—
   " Here comes rack and ruin !"
See, for proof, from roof to roof
   Red flames go leaping.
Loud and high the city's cry;
   Not a soul is sleeping.

On new and old the flames catch hold—
   Windows, doors, gables;
Down go halls, and market stalls,
   Warehouse, wharf, stables.
Belfry clocks and weathercocks
   Topple from their perches;
Wrecked go spire, nave, and choir;
   Gutted lie the churches.

Fierce at feast, like ravenous beast,
   See the fire carouses:
In one night it takes its bite
   Of a thousand houses !

Eighty churches, down they go;
    Beauty past the telling !
Thirteen thousand homes lie low
    Where men once found dwelling.

When was ever known a case
    Of worse desolation ?
How can such a burnt-out place
    Hope for restoration ?
Pity, pity, the great city,
    And the homeless people;
Hollow streets in winding sheets
    Of ash, and shattered steeple !

Yet from strife and storm comes life—
    Birth from death's disguising:
On the walls of old St. Paul's
    New St. Paul's is rising.
And here, there, up in air,
    As the eye searches,
Shine like flowers the shafts and towers
    Of Wren's new churches.

GREAT LIGHTHOUSES

WHENEVER we go to the seaside, about the first thing we notice in the evening are the lights of the lighthouses.

The greatest lighthouse known in the history of the world was also one of the oldest. It was built, more than 2,000 years ago, on the coast of Egypt close to Alexandria, and was called the Pharos.

It was reckoned one of the wonders of the ancient world. The base of it was a great square building containing 300 rooms; from the centre of this rose a tower of eight sides; on the top of that was a round tower; and on the top of all was the beacon which gave light. The whole tower stood higher than the tallest of our English cathedrals. Inside was a spiral slope, going right up to the top, along which donkeys went laden with the firewood for the beacon.

After the Pharos, many other lighthouses

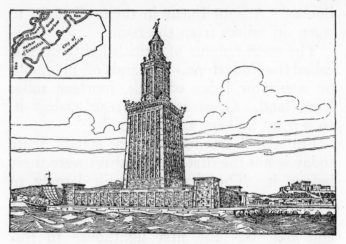

THE PHAROS LIGHTHOUSE.

It was 370 feet high and stood for some 1,600 years (300 B.C. to A.D. 1326). It was the model for the earliest church spire.

were built in other parts of the world. As the nations began to trade with each other across the sea in ships, they found that they needed lights to guide them into each other's harbours; and that is why the towers on which these lights were set are called " lighthouses." When the great Pharos was built, there were very few; now there are thousands of them; and people are still building them.

All round the British Isles we have lighthouses. A light burns in them all night to warn off sailors from the rocks.

The most famous of British lighthouses is called the Eddystone. It stands off Plymouth on a narrow ledge of rock, fourteen miles from land. Great storms break against it, so it must be very strongly built.

But the lighthouse which stands there today is not the first; three others were there before it. The first was built largely of wood about 230 years ago, when William III was King, by a man named Winstanley; and that was the first lighthouse in this country about which anything is known.

He took four years to build it; but it was not strong enough. A year after it was finished, he made the walls twice as thick and added to their height. When that was done he was so proud of his tower that he thought nothing could break it—that it would be safe in any storm. So one day, when a great gale was expected, he went and joined the men who lived in the light-house and looked after it, in order to enjoy the sight of the great seas breaking against his walls.

But the gale became a hurricane, one of

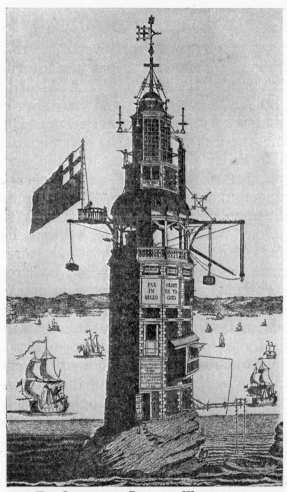

THE LIGHTHOUSE BUILT BY WINSTANLEY.

It was built largely of wood and had galleries and projections.
One day Winstanley, as he was building it, was carried off
by a French ship, as a war was going on with France.

the worst hurricanes that ever came to this country. During the night the hurricane swept the lighthouse away; and Winstanley, its builder, went with it and was never seen again. This happened in the reign of Queen Anne, the last of our Stuart sovereigns.

Winstanley's lighthouse was the first of four great lighthouses — each bigger and stronger than the last—which have been built upon the Eddystone rock. Ever since that day we have gone on building lighthouses; now we have scores and scores of them. If you were to sail in a boat round these islands by night, almost as soon as you lost sight of one lighthouse you would begin to see another. In that way the coast is made safe for ships as they sail at night; they know where they are. The light in some of our lighthouses is so strong that it can be seen for fifty miles. Most lighthouses have what is called a revolving light in them. The light goes round and round, and the beams of it go swinging through the sky like the arms of a windmill.

There is a great lighthouse on the coast of France, the light of which can be clearly seen on the coast of Kent. And when

Englishmen are leaving this country, or returning to it from abroad by night, the last or the first thing they see is one of the lighthouses swinging its light as a signal across the sky.

THE PRESENT LIGHTHOUSE, WHICH IS JUST FIFTY YEARS OLD (1882).

You can guess the height of it from the people standing on the base. In a heavy gale the spray reaches the lantern gallery you see at the top.

THE SEVEN DISOBEDIENT BISHOPS

1688

ON the night of June 30th, 1688, London was lit up with bonfires and rockets and squibs; and in many windows could have been seen a row of seven candles, with one in the centre taller than the rest. The six candles were in honour of six bishops, and the tallest in honour of the Archbishop of Canterbury.

Now this happened towards the end of the short reign of James II, who succeeded his brother Charles II. Unlike most of the people of England, James II was a Roman Catholic, and wishing to bring back England to the Church of Rome, he tried to restore liberty of worship, and in this way to help the Catholics.

But Parliament refused. So, failing to get the law altered, James issued a " Declaration " which allowed what the law forbade; and he ordered the clergy to read it from their pulpits on a certain Sunday in all the churches throughout the land. The clergy refused almost to a man; and the bishops backed them up. Only in four churches in London was the declaration read.

The bishops went even further. The Archbishop of Canterbury summoned to Lambeth as many as could attend; and there, he and six bishops signed a protest which they sent to the King.

"This is rebellion!" cried James II when the protest reached him; and he gave orders for the bishops to be sent for trial in the King's Court. There they were ordered to find £500 as a pledge of their good behaviour during the trial. The bishops refused and were sent to the Tower.

But all London and the greater part of the country were on their side. People cheered them in the streets, and flocked to the Tower in great numbers to ask their blessing. Even Puritan ministers, to whom the Declaration would have granted more liberty than had yet been allowed, approved of what the bishops had done.

Every day the soldiers of the Tower drank to the bishops' health. The Constable of

THE SEVEN BISHOPS ON THEIR WAY TO THE TOWER.
All down the river the Royal Barge containing the bishops
passed between lines of boats, from which arose cries and
shouts of " God bless your Lordships." Notice on the right
the Tower with Traitor's Gate and in the background
London Bridge.

the Tower sent orders that this was not to
be done; but their Captain replied that the
soldiers would drink no other health so long
as the bishops were there.

When the day for their trial approached,
twenty-one of the leading nobles stood bail
for them; and as they came forth from the

Tower, thousands of people crowded round them, cheering and asking their blessing.

They were brought to trial a fortnight later; the jury acquitted them, and they were set free.

Westminster Hall and Palace Yard, and all the streets round about, were thronged with great crowds, who shouted for joy and triumph when the news reached them. Bonfires were lighted, not in London only, but in most of the towns of England, as the word went through the land that the seven disobedient bishops had been acquitted.

King James II himself, in his palace at Whitehall, heard the shouting. "What is that noise?" he asked one of his courtiers. And the courtier replied: "It is only the people shouting because the bishops have been acquitted."

"Only!" exclaimed the King, angry at the news. It was too like the sound of rebellion; and rebellion soon followed: before the year was over King James II was off the throne and had fled the country, never to return to it again.

THE MAN OF FASHION AND
THE PREACHER

1739

BATH is a very beautiful city. It is, indeed, one of the best-built cities in England. It has many streets of well-designed houses, each the work of a single architect, so that from end to end each side looks almost like one building. All this beautiful building was done in the eighteenth century, when Bath became a famous watering-place to which people of rank and fashion came year by year.

Bath owes a great deal of its beauty to a man named Beau Nash, who caused public buildings to be erected, and became a great leader of fashion. Whatever rules he made, the ladies and gentlemen of Bath obeyed them; his word in Bath was law.

Beau Nash lived during six reigns. He was born in Charles II's reign; went to school in James II's reign; to Oxford University in the time of William III; settled

VIEW OF PUMP ROOM, BATH.

at Bath in the reign of Queen Anne; lived there during the reigns of the first two Georges; and died there at the beginning of the reign of George III.

One day Beau Nash had a strange meeting, and a strange experience. He met somebody in the streets of Bath who refused to obey him—a preacher named John Wesley.

At that time Wesley was going all through the country preaching in open places, or at street-corners, or in any building to which he was invited. But though a minister of the Church of England, the churches no longer welcomed him.

Word came to Beau Nash that Wesley was coming to preach in Bath. Beau Nash did not want to have so disturbing a preacher in the city which he ruled so politely and so well; and Wesley was warned beforehand that the great man of Bath was not going to allow him to preach there.

But Wesley came; and finding a large gathering of people waiting to hear him, he began preaching.

He had not been preaching long when up came Beau Nash. He was beautifully dressed; the people made way before him, and then came crowding after, curious to see what would happen.

Beau Nash asked Wesley by whose authority he was preaching. Wesley answered: " By the authority of Jesus Christ, conveyed to me by the Archbishop of Canterbury, when he laid hands upon me and said: ' Take thou authority to preach the Gospel.' "

Nash said that Wesley's preaching frightened people out of their senses. " Sir," inquired Wesley, " have you yourself ever

THE MAN OF FASHION AND THE PREACHER.

heard me preach?" "No." "Then how can you judge of that which you have never heard?" Nash replied that he judged by common report.

" Common report," said Wesley, " is not enough. Your name, sir, is Nash, is it not ? I have heard of you by common report; but I do not think that is enough to judge you by."

Nash was silent for a while, not knowing how to answer; then he said: " I wish to know what all these people have come here for ?"

Then, before Wesley could speak, a woman in the crowd said: " Sir, leave him to me; let an old woman answer him ! You, Mr. Nash, are careful of your body. We are careful of our souls; and it is to find food for our souls that we have come here."

At that, without another word, Beau Nash walked away; and Wesley went on with his preaching.

Many people still go to Bath to look at the city which Beau Nash made so beautiful. But many who go there, go also to look at the entrance of a small alley which is not beautiful at all, but on the steps of which John Wesley stood and preached to the people nearly 200 years ago.

CLIVE IN INDIA

1757

ONE day, in the year 1736, when George II was reigning, the people of Market Drayton saw a small boy climb to the top of the church steeple; and there, straddling a stone spout, he sat, looking down into the market-place.

This boy, who was so troublesome that he had to leave one school after another, was Robert Clive, the man who more than any other caused India to come under British rule.

The English had begun trading with India at the end of Elizabeth's reign; and a company of merchants, called the East India Company, had then been formed.

It was as a clerk of the East India Company that Clive went out to India when he was only eighteen. In those days the voyage to India took from six months to a year; and those who went there were so much cut off from home that they felt as if they had gone into another world.

Clive was so miserable and homesick, that he tried twice to do away with himself; but when, on both occasions, his loaded pistol missed fire, he took it as a sign that he was intended for something better; and though still unhappy, he made up his mind to live.

Before long the chance came for him to make his mark. At that time both Britain and France had trading companies in India; and the two companies were jealous rivals, each trying to get the better of the other. It was from the strife of these two companies that the setting up of British rule in India began. They were constantly fighting; and Clive, liking better to be a soldier than a clerk, entered the army.

He was not very fortunate to begin with. The French, helped by native troops, drove the British out of Madras; and Clive, with other British officers, was taken prisoner. Before long, however, he made his escape; and soon after he became leader in a series of battles which were all successful.

How little he feared death was proved not only in battle. One day he charged a fellow-officer with having cheated at cards. The

THE GUNS FIRING AT PLASSEY.
Notice the uniforms, and the pigtails and the gaiters.

other challenged him to a duel. They met with pistols.

Clive fired and missed. The other came close up to him, and holding his loaded pistol at Clive's head, told him, if he wished to save his life, to take back the charge. Clive answered: " Fire, and be done ! I said you cheated, and I say so still !" At these words the other was so struck by his courage, that he threw his pistol away and granted him his life.

Again and again, in the years that followed,

13

Clive narrowly escaped death, and was always quite fearless. With a mixed force of British and native troops, he won victory after victory for the Indian Princes who favoured the British against the French. Then, at the battle of Plassey (1757), he won a great victory against an army much larger than his own, and from that time onwards British influence in India rapidly grew.

But Clive was not only a successful soldier, he was also a great ruler. He had gone to India as a young man, poor and unknown; he was only forty when he left India for good. Twice in the interval he had returned home. His public service in India covered less than twelve years. Yet, in that short time, by establishing British rule, he changed the future of that great country.

BOY ! COME DOWN !

UP he went into the steeple;
    Word went buzzing through the town.
From the market called the people—
    " Boy ! Boy ! Boy ! Come down !"
High the cry of Market Drayton,
" Oh, you little limb of Satan !
Is it you we have to wait on ?
    Boy ! Boy ! Come down !"

Further far than Market Drayton,
    Facing danger up and down,
Went that " little limb of Satan,"
    Seeking glory and renown.
Many praise while others blame him;
Things he did which stand to shame him,
But for greatness all acclaim him;
Vain that cry which tried to tame him—
    " Boy ! Boy ! Come down !"

WOLFE IN CANADA

1759

TWO years after Clive's great victory of
Plassey in India, a British army of
8,000 men sailed up the river St. Lawrence
in Canada, and pitched its camp on a small
island near the high cliffs on the top of which
stood the strong city of Quebec. In those
days Canada, with Quebec, belonged to the
French. Britain and France were at war.
The British army had come to drive the
French out of Canada.

The city of Quebec stood on a cliff at the
junction of two rivers. It was surrounded
by walls and towers, with batteries of guns,
and was further guarded by a French army
of 14,000 men. How, then, was it possible
for so small an army to take so well-defended
a city ?

The French commander, Montcalm, was
a soldier of high courage and renown. The
English commander, General Wolfe, was sick
and feeble from fever. But on his bed of

sickness he made plans for a victory that seemed impossible. His first attack on the French front had already failed; he had lost 400 of his best men. But the presence of the British Navy on the broad waters of the St. Lawrence gave him the means for moving a large body of troops in safety to another point of landing.

He divided his army; part he left to continue the attack on the French camp, where before it had failed; and part he marched along the southern bank of the river, and put them on board some British ships which had already got past the batteries of the city and were now some miles above it.

When night fell he put some of his men into thirty boats belonging to the ships; and these, floating down the swift current without sound, arrived just before dawn at the point chosen for landing, only a short distance from the city. On the way, however, they were twice seen and challenged by French sentries on the cliffs, but each time an officer answered in perfect French that they were a convoy of provisions, and so the sentry was satisfied.

When they landed, the soldiers had to

climb up a steep slope; but this they did, and surprised and scattered a small French guard which they found on the top of the cliffs. Then came help from the ships which had followed with more troops, and the soldiers also came from the other side of the river.

When the sun rose, the astonished defenders of Quebec saw from their ramparts the long red lines of a British army drawn up on the level ground in the form of battle.

But even now, though the landing had been made, the French had the larger army.

But the British troops were all seasoned men, well used to war; and being confident in their commander, who had already brought them so great a success, they were now sure of victory.

The fight did not last long. Before the steady fire of the British, the troops of the enemy broke and fled. In the course of the fighting, General Wolfe was three times wounded; the third wound was fatal. As he fell he heard one of his officers cry: " They run ! They run !"

" Who run ?" he asked. " The enemy, sir," was the reply. The dying general

WOLFE'S TROOPS CLIMBING THE STEEP SLOPE BEHIND QUEBEC.

This is a modern attempt to show this famous scene: it is part of a film illustrating the History of America, and was made by Yale University, U.S.A.

gave his last order, and then said: " Now God be praised. I die in peace." And so saying he died.

In the same hour, the French leader, Montcalm, fell also.

When the surgeons told him that his wound was fatal, he said: " I am glad of it. I am happy that I shall not live to see Quebec surrender." Before midnight he died, and by his own orders he was buried on the field of battle, in a hole made by a bursting shell.

Five days later, without any more fighting, Quebec gave itself up to the British, and Canada became part of the British Empire. And so, though the numbers who fought in it were small, and though it lasted only a few hours, that battle is reckoned one of the great battles of history, and Wolfe as one of our greatest men.

A GREAT INVENTOR

1767

IN a house belonging to the Free Grammar School of Preston in Lancashire was a parlour hidden by a garden filled with trees. There, two men were working secretly. Two old women, who lived close by, said that they heard in the house a strange humming noise, as if the devil were tuning his bagpipes and the men were dancing a reel. The two men hardly ever went out or in; but now and then there came from the room this low sound of humming, which went on for hours, and then suddenly stopped.

Unable to explain the noise in any other way, the old women thought the two men were practising witchcraft. The story went from mouth to mouth; and so many heard and believed it, that at last they wanted to break in and find out what wickedness was going on there.

Had they done so, they would have found

THE SPINNING-JENNY OF HARGREAVES.

the two men making the first spinning-frame, which one of them, named Richard Arkwright, had invented.

Up till that time cotton-spinning had been done by hand; the work was slow and the output small. Then one day a man called Hargreaves invented the spinning-jenny, which made the work go much quicker; and almost at the same time Richard Arkwright invented a much better machine called the spinning-frame.

These two inventions of more than a century and a half ago helped cotton-spinning to become one of the great industries of England, giving work to hundreds of

By permission of the Town Hall Committee of the Manchester Corporation.   JOHN KAYE ESCAPING.

Kaye invented the "flying-shuttle," which entirely altered the conditions of weaving, thirty years before Hargreaves and Arkwright altered those of spinning. Like Arkwright's invention, that of Kaye was very unpopular; and here Kaye is seen escaping from the mob (who are bursting in at the window); his wife hurried him away concealed in some sheets.

thousands, and supplying cotton goods to the markets of the world.

Richard Arkwright, the inventor of the spinning-frame, began life as a barber. And while he was still in that trade he used to go round the country buying human hair from young girls to make up into wigs; and after dyeing it by a new process which he had discovered, he used to sell it to the wigmakers. Then, as wigs began to go out of fashion, his trade fell away; and he turned his thoughts to the invention of something more valuable. And as he happened to be in that part of the country where cotton-spinning was most done, he gave his mind to improving the spinning.

But when he had invented his machine, he did not at once find the best way to work it. His first spinning machine was worked by horses. Then, as that was too costly, and only gave small results, he tried to work the machine by water-power; and for many years, because his frames were worked by water-power, they were called water-frames. But after a time steam-power came to be used for all kinds of machines.

Though Arkwright's discovery had such

MODERN POWER-DRIVEN WEAVING LOOMS AT WORK. THERE ARE 600 LOOMS IN THIS SHED.
The shuttle of the power-driven loom carries the thread across the loom about 200 times per minute. Compare this with the twenty or thirty throws a skilled hand-loom worker can manage.

great results, and has given work to so many millions of the world's workers, it brought him a lot of trouble. In some of the places the mills which he set up were sacked by rioters, who feared that the new machine would take their work from them; and many of his machines were destroyed.

This great inventor was always a very hard worker. Even at the age of fifty he decided to sleep two hours less, in order to have those hours free to learn grammar and to improve his handwriting. And he regularly worked from five o'clock in the morning till nine at night.

Richard Arkwright had factories in various parts of Great Britain, and in order not to lose more time than he could help, he travelled from one to the other in a vast coach drawn by four horses at a very rapid speed.

His machine was the first which made thread strong enough to make a cloth entirely of cotton. It is to him more than anyone else that we owe the wonderful speed and cheapness in cotton-spinning, which caused it to become, during the next hundred years, one of the greatest industries of our country.

NELSON AT TRAFALGAR

1805

" ENGLAND expects that every man will do his duty !" What is the story of those famous words ?

In the middle of the eighteenth century, Wolfe in Canada and Clive in India had been fighting successfully against the French. Not many years later, the British, with other peoples, were again in arms against the French, whose leader Napoleon was one of the greatest soldiers that ever lived. And the greatest British seaman of that time was Admiral Nelson.

For some months Nelson had been trying to catch the French fleet, and had not caught it. He heard that it had gone to the West Indies. All the way to the West Indies he followed it; but the French managed to escape. At last Nelson had his chance. The French Admiral, named Villeneuve, had joined his fleet to the Spanish, and coming out of the harbour of Cadiz, was met by Nelson off Cape Trafalgar near by.

Now Nelson was not only a great commander, he was also a great sailor. He understood ships and what they could do. And Nelson's plan for the battle of Trafalgar depended as much on the handling and sailing of his ships as on the courage of his men.

In those days all ships sailed by wind. They sailed with it or across it; they could not sail against it. So Nelson made a plan to bring his own fleet into action in such a way that part of the enemy's ships were unable to take an active part in the battle till it was too late. It is said that when, before the battle, Nelson summoned his captains to the flag-ship to explain this plan to them, it was so beautiful and daring, and made victory so sure, that some of them wept for joy.

But it was in the very moment of success, when the French line was broken, that Nelson, standing on the quarter-deck, received his death-wound.

The stars and medals which he wore over his uniform, and had refused to conceal, made him an easy target for the enemy.

THE "VICTORY" IN THE DOWNS IN 1791.

The *Victory* was laid down at Chatham in 1759, the year of Wolfe's victory at Quebec, and was launched in 1765. She mounted 104 guns and had 31 sails, and at Trafalgar went into battle with all her sails set. In a fair breeze she could sail 10 knots=about 11½ land miles in the hour. She is now in Portsmouth Dockyard.

" They have done for me at last !" he cried, as the bullet struck him. " My back-bone is shot through." Then, seeing that an important part of the rigging had been shot away, he ordered it to be replaced.

As they carried him down to the cock-pit, crowded with wounded and dying men, he took out his handkerchief and covered his face and stars, so that the crew might not know their great leader had fallen.

While he lay dying, reports of how the battle was going were constantly brought to him; before long it became clear which side was going to win. Whenever one of the enemy ships that could be seen struck its colours and surrendered, the crew of the *Victory* cheered loudly; and as they cheered, a look of joy came into the face of the dying man.

But Nelson wanted his own captain, Hardy, who was also his greatest friend, to come and tell him the news; but while the fighting was at its worst, Hardy would not leave the deck. More than an hour passed before Hardy could come to him. When at last he entered, Nelson said: " Well, Hardy, how goes the day ?" The captain told him that ten of the enemy's ships had surrendered; but that the van, which the wind had put out of action, was tacking to get back, and would soon be within gun-range. But now that hardly mattered, the battle was already decided.

" I hope," said Nelson, " that none of our own ships have struck ?" " Not one," replied Hardy.

Then, and not till then, did Nelson speak of himself. " I am a dead man, Hardy," he said. " I am going fast: it will be over soon." Hardy was then obliged to leave him: in fifty minutes he came back again. Complete victory was now certain: at least fifteen of the enemy's ships had surrendered. "That is well," said Nelson; "but I bargained for twenty."

He was now near his end; but his thoughts were still for the safety of his fleet. He knew that a storm was brewing, and that for disabled ships to be at close quarters together in a storm would be dangerous. " Anchor, Hardy, anchor !" he cried. And again, in a louder voice, he insisted that the fleet should anchor.

Then his strength sank, and he spoke low.

" Don't throw me overboard," he said. He wished to be taken home, and buried beside his parents, unless the nation willed otherwise. Once more his captain and friend had to leave him. " Kiss me, Hardy!" he said, as they parted. Hardy kissed him on the cheek, and went back to the deck.

They did not meet again. Three hours and a quarter after he had received his wound, Nelson died. " I have not been a *great* sinner," he said to the chaplain. " Thank God, I have done my duty," were his last words.

" Duty " was the word which Nelson had chosen in sending out his battle signal before the battle began: " England expects that every man will do his duty." The phrase has become famous. There is a curious story attached to it. In drawing up the signal, Nelson had first used his own name. " Nelson expects——" One of his officers asked would not " England " be better ? Nelson at once agreed; and so the famous signal has passed into history.

During the long wars with Napoleon, what most saved England from invasion and defeat was the British Navy.

Every time that the French hoped to win victory through the strength of their navy, it was broken and beaten by the British fleet under Nelson and other admirals.

Nelson's last and greatest victory of all was this battle of Trafalgar (1805), in which so large a number of French ships were destroyed that, after that day, the British fleet was not again challenged to battle—till the last Great War.

THE BOWS OF THE " VICTORY."
Notice the three tiers of guns.

THE SURRENDER OF NAPOLEON

1815

TWO small midshipmen were watching from the *Bellerophon*, one of His Majesty King George III's famous battleships, a crowd of boats lying alongside. One of the boats, containing a fat old gentleman with a very large hat, was holding on to the King's ship by a rope. The midshipmen, waiting for their chance, suddenly pulled the rope tight, and off went the fat gentleman's hat into the sea !

From the deck above, the most famous man then living was watching the scene ; and he laughed loudly. It was the only time he laughed in what was to him the saddest of all his journeys. It was the great Napoleon.

Shortly before this, when the *Bellerophon* was lying off the coast of France, Napoleon having been defeated at Waterloo, near Brussels, had come to place himself under the protection of the British nation. A French brig, with the Emperor on board, lay near at hand; a barge had gone over from the *Bellerophon* to fetch him.

In a few minutes the ship's crew, as they watched, saw a small man in a grey coat and a three-cocked hat stepping quickly down into the boat. The boat pushed off. The captain of the *Bellerophon* gave orders for a guard of marines to stand aft on the quarter-deck, ready to receive Napoleon with the honours due not to an Emperor, but only to a general. For as an Emperor he was no longer to be recoginsed—those were the orders of the British Government.

So when Napoleon stepped on board—the greatest soldier in history, the man who had conquered half Europe and brought to France her greatest glory—the captain of the *Bellerophon* only touched his hat, and did not take it off as he would have done to anyone of royal rank.

The Emperor appeared not to notice. He took off his hat—a thing he would not always have done to great princes—and said: " I come to place myself under the protection of your King and your laws." The Captain then turned and conducted him to his cabin. Napoleon, who had expected to be treated as a guest of honour, found himself a prisoner. Never again was he to be free.

Early next morning, as the ship was rounding Cape Ushant and leaving the coast of France behind, a midshipman saw Napoleon come on deck. The deck, still wet from being washed, was slippery. Napoleon stumbled and almost fell; the midshipman took off his hat and gave him his arm. Climbing the poop-ladder by the boy's aid, he went forward, and mounting a gun-slide, drew out a telescope. And there, from five in the morning till mid-day, he stood watching the coast of France as it disappeared, looking for the last time at the land to which he had first brought so much glory and at last final defeat.

When the land had become only a speck, he turned and saw his faithful servant, a man named Bertrand, waiting to help him down. He spoke not a word; and as he walked he tottered and stumbled; his head hung heavily forward, so that his face could not be seen. He disappeared into his cabin.

The captain and the crew took a great

NAPOLEON ON BOARD THE "BELLEROPHON."

The *Bellerophon* had a wonderful fighting record; "no one," it was said, "can be a coward on board the *Bellerophon*." At the battle of Trafalgar she was at one time or other engaged by eight or nine of the enemy's ships. The sailors called her "old Billy Ruff'n." Napoleon suffered little during the voyage from sea-sickness; but one of his followers who had put on a French naval uniform was very ill, and Napoleon told him to take his uniform off as he was a disgrace to the French navy!

fancy to him. " Well," said one of the crew, " they may abuse that man as much as they please, but if the people of England knew him as well as we do, they would not touch a hair of his head !"

Six years later he died in lonely exile on the island of St. Helena in the Atlantic Ocean, to which he had been sent a prisoner by the British. He was one of the greatest conquerors the world has ever known; and yet he had failed. His reign and his power were over. But the mark he left on history was as great as that of any man who had lived before him.

In his will he expressed the wish that his body might lie in Paris " on the banks of the Seine in the midst of the French people whom he had loved so well." Twenty years after his death the wish was granted; and he lies now under a high dome in a splendid tomb, which is guarded night and day by two sentries, as a token of the great honour in which his memory is held by the French nation.

SWIFT NICK AND THE HIGHWAYS

SWIFT NICK AND THE HIGHWAYS

IN the days of Nelson and Napoleon
there were no trains. In the olden times,
before railways came in, everybody travelled
by road; and it took days for people to go
distances which we now cover in a few hours.

In our Stuart period, before roads in
Britain were properly made, the average rate
at which coaches travelled was only three
and a half miles an hour. Even in the
great coaching days, only a hundred years
ago, the fastest mail-coach took two days to
go from London to Edinburgh.

In those days, and for a good while after,
the upkeep of the roads was paid for by toll-
gates, called "turnpikes," which stood at
intervals along the main roads; and all people
riding or driving had to pay before being
allowed to pass through. Many of the little
toll-houses in which the toll-keepers lived
can still be seen; but the gates are gone.

Those who have read the eighteenth-

century story of John Gilpin will remember
how the turnpike men, thinking that he rode
a race, threw open their gates at his coming,
so that he need not stop.

Now while the roads and coaches were
the only general means of travel, there was
always danger from highwaymen, especially
in the eighteenth century, when trade and
wealth had much increased, and men of
business were constantly going to and fro
between town and town. And though, for
greater safety, the coach guard carried a gun
called a blunderbuss, the coach was often
stopped by armed highwaymen wearing
masks, so that their faces might not be seen;
and the passengers were robbed of their
watches, jewelry and purses.

The highwaymen were generally quite nice
about it, and behaved otherwise like gentlemen. They were not rough or violent;
sometimes they were even kind, and would
return to the passengers enough money to
let them finish their journey.

But however nicely the highwaymen behaved, if they were caught they were hanged.

The highwaymen had wonderful horses.
There is a story of Charles II's reign of

Two Highwaymen stopping a Traveller.

how a highwayman, named Swift Nick, rode for his life on his horse from London to York. A popular ballad tells of his virtues:

" He maintained himself like a gentleman,
Bes'des he was good to the poor;
He rode about like a bold hero,
And gained himself favour therefor."

There is another legend which says that another highwayman, Dick Turpin, did the same thing a hundred years later on his famous horse " Black Bess "; and that he jumped all the gates on his horse; and at the end of the journey she fell dead—190 miles in fifteen hours !

It is not surprising that there was so much robbery on the high-roads in the country. At that time there were no proper police; and the roads often ran for many miles through lonely places with not a house by the way. But it is strange to read now how close to London, and even in London streets, highwaymen were able to ply their trade and get away uncaught. Even the highest people in the land were sometimes their victims.

One day King George II was walking in Kensington Gardens, when a single highwayman climbed over the wall and robbed him of his purse, his watch and his buckles. The man was very respectful and apologetic, and said that he would not have done such a thing to the King's majesty had he not been in great distress for money.

About fifty years later the Prince of Wales and his brother, the Duke of York, were robbed in a street out of Berkeley Square, close to Piccadilly. And in both these cases of robbery from royal persons the men got away.

Most people would say that our high-roads are safe now; but they would be quite mistaken. For while in the old days a few

people here and there were killed by highwaymen, now with our furious driving of
motor-cars we kill hundreds. And nobody
is hanged for it!

THE COACH-DRIVERS.

This is a political picture showing two rival statesmen, one,
the great Chatham, urging on the horses, and the other,
Bute, the first Scot who ever became Prime Minister,
trying to hold them in. The picture shows a carriage of
the eighteenth century, with the basket behind for extra
passengers.

THE "ROCKET."

It was painted yellow and black, with a white chimney, and reached a speed of 29 miles an hour. The engine was slightly altered before the opening of the Liverpool and Manchester line in 1830, when it ran 11 miles at 36 miles an hour.

THE FIRST
RAILWAY

1825

ON September 27th, 1825, an enormous crowd might have been seen near Darlington in Durham. They had come to see the opening of the first real railway in the world, and the first train; and not a few had come expecting to see the engine blow up. The engine had been built by a man named George Stephenson, and it can still be seen in Darlington Station.

It was a great event in the history of this country when the first steam railway was made, and the first passenger train ran over it. That happened twenty years after Nelson's death at Trafalgar, and ten years after Napoleon's defeat at Waterloo.

What kind of man was he who built the first steam engine that would move about and draw a passenger train ?

George Stephenson was the son of a fireman of a colliery engine, earning twelve shillings a week. There were six children, but the parents were careful and hard-working. We are also told that they found great joy in animals, especially birds.

When George found work at twopence a day as a cowboy on a farm, he used to amuse himself by making models of engines in clay, using hemlocks for steam pipes. But he badly wanted to be an engine man; and great was his joy when, at fourteen years of age, he was made assistant fireman at a colliery with a wage of a shilling a day. He was very strong, and very fond of lifting heavy weights.

Later, he worked a pumping engine and earned twelve shillings a week. " Now I am a made man for life !" he told his friends.

He was nearly eighteen years old before he learnt to read. It was the time when Napoleon was winning his great victories in Europe, and there was no one so anxious to learn about Napoleon's deeds as the young engine man working in the colliery. So he

14

saved some money, went to a night school, and took lessons in spelling and reading at a cost of threepence a week. And it was a proud day for him when, at the age of nineteen, he was able to write his own name.

At the age of twenty-seven he was working the engines of a colliery. While doing so, he took his engine to pieces every Saturday, so that he might learn thoroughly how it was made. He became so skilled with engines that he was known as the " engine doctor." At the age of thirty he was earning £100 a year. At night he used to mend watches and clocks to help pay for his son's schooling.

Having now better wages and more leisure, he began working out his great invention, namely a steam engine that could move about from place to place by its own power, and draw a train with carriages. His first moving engine he made for use in a colliery; but with a load of thirty tons of coal it could only go at four miles an hour. That was not good enough. He tried again, and made another which did much better.

Then, in 1823, some business men of Darlington, in the county of Durham, decided to make a railway of twenty-five miles

TRAVEL SOME HUNDRED YEARS AGO.

On the right is a steam-carriage, which is the first sort of motor-car. On the left is a coach with four horses, who are shying at a man on a hobby-horse, the forerunner of the bicycle. In the background, on the left, is a paddle-steamer which is using sail as well, and on the right an early railway train. In the air is an early airship.

from Darlington to Stockton-on-Tees; and George Stephenson was appointed engineer. For this railroad Stephenson built the steam engine which drew a train carrying not only luggage wagons, but passengers too.

On September 27th, 1825, the engine started on its first run with a long and heavy train load behind it: twelve luggage wagons laden with coal and other produce, twenty-one open wagons filled with passengers, and one covered coach containing the directors of the railway company. In front went a horseman with a flag to warn people off the line, and Stephenson himself was the engine-driver.

Before the train had gone half a mile Stephenson was quite sure that it could go much faster than it was going, in spite of its heavy load. He told the horseman to get out of the way, and he put on steam; the speed increased, and the first train travelled on to Darlington at the rate of fifteen miles an hour.

Everybody cheered; hats were waved. The engine was a success; it was a great day for England.

A few years later Stephenson had made another engine called the " Rocket," which

STEPHENSON'S FIRST RUN.

could go at the rate of thirty-five miles an hour. Engines can now go more than twice as fast, and can draw far heavier loads.

Stephenson's first passenger railway was only twenty-five miles long, and there was then only one engine and one train. Now, if we look at a map of the railroads of England, they are so many and so close together that it looks like a badly made spider's web. In England alone there are now 19,822 miles of railroad.

But it was George Stephenson, the fireman's son, who, by making the first engine that could move by rail and draw a train load of passengers, was the real father of the railway system of the world.

THE " FLYING SCOTSMAN " ON ITS WAY TO SCOTLAND.

THE GREAT TREK

1835-1836

IN the year 1835 a small boy of the age of ten could have been seen riding in an ox-wagon across the wilds lying north of Cape Colony. He was taking part in a long and perilous journey known as the Great Trek. This small boy became a famous man in later years. His people were Dutch farmers, whom we call Boers.

A number of Dutch farmers and traders had settled at the Cape of Good Hope in South Africa nearly three hundred years ago —when Charles I was King of England.

Later, during the war against Napoleon, the Cape was occupied by the British. At the end of the war, the British bought the Cape from the Dutch, and it has ever since remained a part of the British Empire.

But the Dutch, not liking English ways and customs, began moving northwards to the wilder lands which were still held by native tribes. They went inland and north, trying thus to keep for themselves their own ways.

This movement of the Boer farmers was called " trekking." It began more than a hundred years ago, and was always going on here and there, as the British Colony grew in numbers and strength.

But the biggest movement of all, which was called the " Great Trek," took place in the years 1835-36, just before Victoria became Queen of England. Then several thousands of Boers made up their minds that they would have a new country of their own, and govern it in their own way. So they sold their houses and farms; and taking their wives and children and slaves with them, they turned their faces to the north, and set out to find for themselves a new land.

It was something like the Exodus of the Children of Israel from Egypt. They brought out the great lumbering ox-wagons, and into these they packed their wives and their little ones, and all the family goods and furniture which they could find room for. Harnessing to each wagon long teams

BOERS ON THE GREAT TREK.

of oxen, they journeyed out from the farms in which they had spent all their lives, driving beside them their herds of cattle and sheep, to start new farms in the land lying to the north.

That great trek was the beginning of two new states—the Orange Free State and the Transvaal.

Among the children who rode in these ox-wagons on the Great Trek was a small boy, aged ten, named Paul Kruger, who, later on, was the ruler of the Boers in the Transvaal. Kruger died in exile, and he did not live long enough to see the old quarrel between Boer and British brought to a happy end in the " Union " of the Colonies of South Africa.

NATIVES MAKING A MOTOR ROAD IN SOUTH AFRICA.

THE LADY OF THE LAMP

1854-1856

" SUCH a head !" said Queen Victoria when she saw the Lady of the Lamp. " I wish we had her at the War Office !"

Who was the Lady of the Lamp ? Her name was Florence Nightingale. She was the daughter of rich parents and was well-educated. She was a woman of strong will and great energy. For ten years she studied nursing. Then, when the call of duty came to her, she offered her services to the country.

Britain was at war with Russia in the Crimea. The war was being managed badly at the front, and the hospitals at the base were being managed worse. The suffering in the big hospital was greater than the suffering which had to be borne on the field of battle. The hospital was so understaffed and so badly run that nursing could hardly be said to exist. There was no system, no cleanliness; the wounded lay in filth and misery, and died like flies.

Florence Nightingale came out from England with a staff of women nurses and altered everything.

When the stores which she had asked for were refused, she took a hatchet and broke open the store-house door, and helped herself to what she needed.

Before long, under her rule, the hospital became a changed place.

The soldiers loved her; the orderlies obeyed her; the officials feared her. She worked so hard that often she was on her feet for twenty out of the twenty-four hours. When all the rest of her staff had gone off duty, she would be seen going round with her lamp from bed to bed, taking a last look at the hundreds of sick men who lay in her charge. Her mere presence seemed to have a healing effect on them; they kissed her shadow as she passed. There was no coarseness, no swearing: the place which had been so like hell had become almost like heaven.

She gave orders, but never raised her voice; and her orders were obeyed. A doctor once said to her that something could

Florence Nightingale in a Ward of the Hospital for those Wounded in the Crimea.

not be done. "It must be done," she replied. And done it was.

Before her work was finished she herself fell ill of a fever, and was very near to death. But when she was well enough to be moved she would not go. Not while the sick and wounded soldiers still needed her would she return to England. She went back at last, broken in health.

Florence Nightingale lived on to the age of ninety, always at work for the improvement of hospital nursing.

Her statue now stands by the side of the Crimea Memorial in one of the chief London streets; and it is as "The Lady of the Lamp" that we see her there: tall, stately and serene, carrying a lamp in her hand.

AUSTRALIA'S BRAVE EXPLORERS

1770-1862

MORE than six hundred years ago the famous traveller Marco Polo,[1] when living in China, heard tell of a great land lying south across the sea. Nobody knew anything about it, only that it was there, and that it was very big. Some centuries later, a map, on which a large southern land is shown, was made in the reign of Henry VIII and dedicated to him.

This land was Australia. After that men knew that it existed. But it was not till the year 1770, in George III's reign, that Captain Cook, the great explorer, landed upon its eastern coast at a place called Botany Bay.

This name was given to it because such a number of new plants were found there growing in great variety; it was like a botanical garden of strange flowers run wild.

[1] See page 244.

A few years later came settlers from England; and the first English colony was founded round the great harbour which is now called Sydney.

But for many years after that, though the colony grew, and though other colonies and trading stations were set up along the coast, the colonists knew little of the country inland. Australia was not really discovered; people just lived on the edge of it, and that was all.

Then, about a hundred years ago, men began to explore the interior. They crossed the range of Blue Mountains which lay west of Sydney; and on the other side, they found not waterless desert as they had expected, but pleasant fertile country suitable for farms and flocks. Going further, they found rivers, not running down to the sea, but away from it, inland. After that they began to explore in all directions; and some of the greatest travels ever made, in which much hardship and suffering were borne, were undertaken by the men who set out to cross Australia from east to west, or from south to north.

The greatest and one of the first of these explorers was Captain Charles Sturt. Believing that an inland sea was waiting to be discovered, he set out to find it. His first travels took place during a season that was very hot and dry. The river whose course he set out to follow shrank gradually into a wilderness of dry reeds; the ground was so parched and hot that the hoofs of his horses broke on it; he journeyed for days and days without water for man or beast; and when at last he came to a wide river he found that it was salt. And so he failed to reach his end, and returned to the starting-point.

But again and again Sturt and others set out to explore in different directions—west, and south and north. One by one they found the great rivers of Australia. The greatest of all, which is called the Murray, Captain Sturt discovered in 1830. Then other rivers were discovered, further north and west, which do not run into the sea at all, but into great inland lakes, some of which are more than 100 miles long.

Further inland and to the north lay great stretches of sandy desert; and across this desert the explorers tried many times to make their way, but again and again they failed. Sturt, going first where others fol-

AUSTRALIAN COLONISTS CROSSING A RIVER IN BASKET
BOATS A HUNDRED YEARS AGO.

lowed later, was never able to get even half-way. Dense scrub, and poisonous nettles, and terrible thorns, and salt water kept turning him back. Sometimes he and his companions had to go for over 100 miles through dry, waterless tracts, carrying their water with them. When they came upon signs of water they had to dig deep to find it below the surface; and once for five days their horses had to go without any at all.

During another time of terrible heat and drought, they came, almost at the last gasp,

AN AUSTRALIAN NATIVE
RIDING A TURTLE.

on a spring of water rising from under a rock; and there they stayed for six months, unable to go further, unable to go back. To escape from the heat they dug themselves a cave in the ground; but even that became like an oven. Wood and metal were so hot in the sun that, when they touched them, their hands were blistered; and when Sturt sat down to write his diary the ink dried in his pen.

But even so, they made fresh discoveries; and more and more they found that Australia had it in great fertile tracts, crossed by rivers, where white men could live.

Sometimes, as they made their way to these places, they were in great danger from the black natives, or bushmen, who lay in wait for them on the banks of the rivers; and more than one explorer, falling into their hands, was killed and eaten; for many of the bushmen of Australia were cannibals.

So difficult was the country, and so great were the distances of desert without water which had to be crossed, that not till 1862 did any man try to cross Australia from south to north, and live to tell of it. Two men, named Burke and Wills, with two others to help them, had got across the year before, using for the first time camels as well as horses for the journey. But having reached the coast, they missed the relief party which should have met them there; and worn out by hardship and starvation, neither Burke nor Wills lived to tell the story of that great adventure.

And so it happened that another explorer, named Stuart, was the first man who lived to reap the reward and the fame for which others also had so bravely striven. Three times he made the attempt and twice he failed; the first time he came within 400 miles of his journey's end; the second time within 150 miles. The third time, after a journey of several months, starting from Adelaide in the south, he came in 1862 to a place on the shores of the Indian Ocean in the far north, now known as Port Darwin. And there, going down into the water, he dipped his feet, and washed his hands in the sea, as he had promised a friend that he would do if ever he succeeded in reaching it.

On the very day when he returned to Adelaide in triumph, the bodies of the two brave men, Burke and Wills, who had died in making the attempt, were being carried through the streets for burial.

Of Stuart's great exploit they share the fame; but because Stuart lived to tell the story, his name is the better known.

And one of the things told by Stuart of what happened on his second journey is well

AN AUSTRALIAN NATIVE CHILD FEEDING A KANGAROO IN NORTHERN AUSTRALIA.

worth telling again, for it is very beautiful. As he passed through the thick "bush" inhabited only by black tribes, he came upon a small canoe, beautifully made and covered with native carving. The canoe was not lying on the ground, it was wedged into the branches of a tree; and in the canoe, which was only thirty inches long, lay the body of a small child. The bushmen of Australia were a primitive and savage people, and many of their customs were horrible; yet in that burial of a little child, in a canoe hung on a tree, there is a sort of beauty. It seems as if they could not have given it so beautiful a cradle in death, unless they had also loved it.

SONG

Hush-a-bye, Baby
  On the tree-top;
When the wind blows,
  The cradle will rock.
When the bough breaks,
  The cradle will fall;
But the Baby asleep
  Will know nothing at all.

And nobody knows
  Who the Baby can be!
And, when the wind blows,
  (Oh, pretty to see!)
Nobody knows
  Why there in a boat,
Up in a tree-top
  They left him to float!

A GREAT MISSIONARY

1813-1878

ONE day in the year 1871 an explorer named Stanley, coming to a native village in the unknown wilds of Africa, heard a voice speak to him in English. " Good-morning, sir." Stanley turned round in great surprise, and saw a black man smiling at him. " Who the mischief are you ?" inquired Stanley. " I am, sir, the servant of Dr. Livingstone," replied the black man.

How was it that these two white men happened to be in the wilds of Africa ?

A hundred years ago little was known about Africa except the countries lying round the coast. It was called the " Dark Continent "; what the centre of it was like nobody knew. Then, into the very heart of it, went a man named David Livingstone; and with him began the great work, which others have carried on after him, of discovering the interior of Africa, with its lakes and rivers, its many millions of people, and its strange wild beasts, some of which had never been known before.

Livingstone at the age of ten entered a cotton mill. Although he had to be at the mill at six o'clock in the morning, he used to attend an evening school; and he continued to read in the mill by fixing his book on the spinning-jenny. He was keen on reading about flowers and animals and rocks, and he spent his holidays in searching for nature specimens. Then he went to Glasgow University, and paid his way by working for half the year in the factory, and the other half studying and attending lectures.

He took his medical degree, and at the age of twenty-seven was sent as a missionary to Africa. Before long his work of setting up mission-stations forced him to make long journeys into the interior: he began to explore. His chief reason for this was that he hoped to find some high tableland where he might set up a healthy mission-station, free from the terrible diseases to which all who lived in the swamps and forests were subject. Once, in his adventures, he was badly bitten by a lion, so badly that he bore the marks and the pain of it for the rest of his life.

But he was bitten much more often by the tsetse fly, which is the greatest pest of Africa, and is the cause of " sleeping sickness " from which so many die. It was to find some place free from the tsetse fly that Livingstone started to explore.

As he went into the interior he found slavery everywhere. The sufferings of the natives were terrible; and the trade in slaves was practised not only by the black people themselves. The Portuguese settlers also encouraged it, as other Europeans have done since, finding that slavery is the easiest way of securing cheap labour for work which Europeans cannot do themselves.

Livingstone saw that the only way to stop slavery in Africa was to open up the interior of the country to trade, and to bring into it people who would not allow slavery for themselves, however much it might profit them. And so, this way and that he went, exploring the " Dark Continent," preparing the way for others to follow; and wherever he stayed the natives learned to love and trust him. Once, when he had to move to another place, the whole tribe amongst whom he had been working went with him.

LIVINGSTONE AND THE LION.

The lion shook Livingstone as a terrier does a rat, but then
    left him to attack the man with the gun, who tried to
    shoot him, but the gun missed fire.   Finally, a man with
    a spear came to the rescue, and other bullets also took effect
    on the lion.

One day, following the course of a river
that is called the Zambesi, he came to some
great falls—the greatest falls in the world, higher
than the Falls of Niagara—and these he named
after his Queen, the Victoria Falls, the name
by which they have been known ever since.

Livingstone also discovered some of the
great lakes which lie in the centre of Africa,
and the sources of many of its rivers.   Twice
he came back to England, bringing with him
reports of his great discoveries.   When going out

a third time, he was lost sight of; no news came from him; people feared that he was dead.

They became so anxious that a search party was sent out under another famous explorer named Stanley. After a long search Stanley found him, a solitary white man, sick and feeble, living among the natives, and tended by faithful black servants who had learned to love him.

Livingstone was sick and half-starved, but quite cheerful, and still bent on going on with the work to which he had given his life. He refused to leave it and come home. Stanley supplied him with most of the things which he so badly needed, and there left him.

A year later he died. One day his servants came into his room and found him kneeling by his bed. He had died quite peacefully at his prayers.

His faithful servants took out his heart and buried it under a tree in the place where he had died. His body was taken to England, and now lies in Westminster Abbey, under a stone bearing his name.

To some Scottish children he once gave this motto: " Fear God and work hard "—as indeed he himself did all his life.

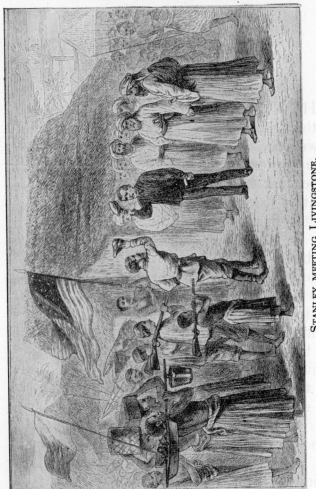

STANLEY MEETING LIVINGSTONE.

" Dr. Livingstone, I presume," were the first words uttered by Stanley when he found Livingstone. Notice the American flag, as Stanley was sent out by an American newspaper.

A GREAT PRESIDENT

1809-1865

THE United States of America have as their head not a King but a President.

Two very great men have been Presidents of the United States.

The first was George Washington, who fought in George III's reign to free America from the British Crown. And when America won, he became the first President of the Republic.

The other was Abraham Lincoln, who was the son of a settler in the backwoods of America. He was born in a log-cabin which his father had built for himself and his family. The father could hardly read or write; but the mother taught her son to read. As they were too poor to afford candles, young Abraham used to sit reading by the light of the log-fire all the books he could get. Among the books that he loved were *Pilgrim's Progress*, *Robinson Crusoe*, and *Æsop's Fables*, and it was from such books as these that he learned to speak and write English so well. He would often do sums at night before the fire, using a piece of wood for a slate.

His mother died when he was ten years old, and soon after, his father, wishing to find a second wife, left his three small children to look after themselves in the log-cabin and live as best they could. He was away for three months; then he came back, bringing a new wife with three children of her own; and with her help, and the hard work of Abraham and his sister, the enlarged family grew and prospered.

But though a worker, Abraham Lincoln was always a great reader. He began also to train himself for public speaking; and going out alone into the forest, he would speak to the trees as though they were living people. As he grew up he became very tall; he was four inches over six feet, long in the leg and very thin, but also very strong. He had huge hands, and such a reach of arm that in wrestling and fighting no one was able to beat him.

Now in those days, in all the Southern States of America, slavery was allowed, but in the North it was forbidden. And the people of America were divided into two parties; one party wanted slavery to be done away with in all the States; the other party wanted it to be allowed everywhere. Those living in the South were for slavery, most of those living in the North were against it.

Lincoln was still quite a young man when, taking a voyage down the Mississippi from north to south, he came to some of the slave States, and saw women slaves being flogged. He began speaking against slavery; he spoke well, better than anyone else. Before long he became the leader of those who wished to see the end of slavery. And though he saw it would be difficult to get rid of slavery in the States in which it had long existed, he objected strongly to slaves being allowed in any of the new States, because he wanted these to be homes, not for black men working in slavery, but for free poor people of the white races to better their condition.

But presently there came a new danger. The Southern States said that, if slavery was ended, they would separate from the Northern States and be a nation by themselves. Lincoln believed that for America to be thus divided would be a greater evil than slavery;

ABRAHAM LINCOLN.

but there was one thing on which he and nearly all in the Northern States were agreed —slavery must not be extended into any State where it did not already exist.

Before long the quarrel grew so hot that the Southern States began arming themselves and preparing to separate. Civil war seemed near. Lincoln was now taking an active part in these affairs. The strength of his character, his patience, his firm will, his cool judgment, made men put trust in him.

When the quarrel was at its height, his fame had become so great that he was chosen to be President. Hardly had this happened when the Southern States committed an act of war: a fort held by government troops was fired upon and forced to surrender. That was the beginning of Civil War in America, which began in 1861 and went on until 1865.

At first the South got the better of it; but presently, when Lincoln had got rid of generals who did not know how to lead an army, and had put better ones in their places, the Northern States became victorious; and at last the whole of the Southern army surrendered and the war was over.

But while the war had been going on, Lincoln had come to the conclusion that slavery could no longer be allowed in any part of the United States. In the second year of the war he declared freedom for all slaves throughout America.

In the year when the war ended he was again chosen to be President, only a few

AN AUCTION IN NEW ORLEANS.
In the centre some slaves are being sold.

weeks before the final victory. A month
later he was shot dead by a madman while
he was watching a play in the theatre at
Washington.

Word went through America that " Father
Abraham," as his people loved to call him,
was dead. The news came to the army. An
officer opened the despatch. One who was
there has left an account of what followed:

15

" I never before found myself in a mass of men overcome by emotion. Ten thousand soldiers were sobbing together."

It was a great tribute to a great man. Civil war is of all kinds of war the most terrible, and the wounds it leaves are the hardest to heal. But though Lincoln was the chosen leader of one side of a divided people, he had so beautiful a character, and was so generous in mind and action toward the defeated, that before long his memory was reverenced by the whole nation—North and South alike.

He is still the most loved and revered of all the American Presidents.

A GREAT LIFE-SAVER

1822-1895

WHEN a great general wins a battle, it is mainly for the benefit of his own country. But when a man of science makes a great discovery, it does good to the whole world.

So it matters little whether the discovery is made by an Englishman, a Frenchman, a German or an American. We ought all to feel just as grateful to the one as to the other, since all nations alike get the good of it.

And that is why we all honour the name of a great French doctor named Louis Pasteur. He was the son of a tanner who had served in the army of Napoleon. When he was sixteen, Louis was sent to school in Paris. But his health broke down, and he longed for home: " If I could smell a tannery once more," he said, " I should feel well."

When he grew up he saved the great wine industry of France from ruin, and by doing so, hundreds of poor families could earn their daily bread again. Not only that; but he also saved the lives of many thousands of men, women, and children from death.

What was it that Pasteur discovered that had such great results ? He discovered that some diseases were caused by some very small forms of life—or " germs "; before that no one had guessed there could be life in anything so small. Though germs are necessary and some do so much good that man could not live without them, others can also do much harm.

Now France is a great wine country. It has thousands of vineyards, and many of the people make their living by growing vines. But when Pasteur was a young man, the wine-growers were in great trouble: a disease had got into the wine; it went bad and would not keep, and it seemed as if the wine trade and the workers in it would be ruined.

Pasteur discovered how this disease was caused, and how to cure it. That was his first great discovery; it saved the vineyards

THE ALSATIAN SHEPHERD BOY AND THE MAD DOG.

from going to waste and the vine-growers from ruin.

But the most famous of all Pasteur's discoveries was the cure for the disease which follows the bite of a mad animal. He found out the cause of the disease, and how to cure it.

The first patient to be cured by this new process was an Alsatian shepherd boy who had been bitten by a mad dog. Pasteur had cured animals of this disease, but he did not like to take the risk with human beings. But the boy's mother had great faith in the famous doctor. " If you can cure animals, you can cure my boy," she said, and the great doctor did cure her boy.

Dr. Pasteur was a very hard worker. And if he had kept all his discoveries to himself he might have become the wealthiest man in the world. " I could never work for money," he once said, " but I could always work for science."

Once he came over to England to attend a meeting in London. News came that he was arriving in the hall, and as he entered there was a great outburst of cheering. " It is no doubt the Prince of Wales arriving," said Pasteur, turning to the friend beside him.

" No; it is you they are all cheering," replied the friend; for Pasteur, the most modest of men, could not believe the cheering was meant for him.

No wonder that Pasteur's own people, the French, honour him above all others. They were once asked to name their greatest countrymen; and they put Pasteur, the great healer, first, and Napoleon, the great soldier and ruler, second.

THE CHILDREN'S FRIEND

Lord Shaftesbury lived from 1801 to 1885

A HUNDRED years ago the life of children was very different from what it is now. Today, as we all know, children can go to free schools as soon as they are five years old, and remain there till they are at least fourteen. But a hundred years ago very few children went to school at all, and as early as five years old they might have to work in the mines and factories for twelve or even fourteen hours a day, for only a few pence a week.

The children had no playtime. They were taught nothing. Some worked in factories. Others worked in the dark mines half-starved and half-naked, dragging loaded trucks like pit-ponies, and lifting heavy weights, which made them grow up twisted and deformed. In some of the coal-mines were children only four or five years old, doing various kinds of work with their tiny

456

hands for as many hours a day as the men and women.

All that child-labour has gone now. The man more than all others who brought it to an end was Lord Shaftesbury, a land-owner of Dorset. He forced people to know what was going on in those factories and underground places, and made his country-men ashamed of it. First he got a law passed through Parliament forbidding children or women to go down and work in the mines at all. Then he got the hours of labour, in places where they still did work, shortened to ten hours a day.

From that he went on to make things better for the poor children living in the slums of our great cities. Of one of these children Lord Shaftesbury wrote:

" I recollect the case of a boy who, during last winter, passed the greater part of his nights in the iron roller of Regent's Park. He climbed every evening over the railings and slipped to his shelter, where he lay in some sort of comfort."

Lord Shaftesbury and others took much interest in Ragged Schools where the very poorest could be taught free. These schools grew and grew until thousands came to them. Twenty years after they had been started, Lord Shaftesbury said: " I would rather be Head of the Ragged Schools than have the command of armies."

Such schools went on till better schools with free education were provided for all. But Lord Shaftesbury never stopped work; as soon as one good thing had been set going, he started on another. Nearly always he had against him people who made money out of the evils he was trying to get rid of; and nearly always he won. The people of this country began to know that any cause for which he spoke and worked was a cause which needed looking into.

One of the most cruel occupations for little boys at this time was to climb up narrow chimneys, sometimes only a foot wide, and sweep them. Lord Shaftesbury told Parliament that he himself knew of a child at that moment (1834) of four and a half years, and another of six years, employed in sweeping chimneys. But many laws had to be passed before that evil came to an end.

Lord Shaftesbury was also a friend of shoe-blacks and street-costers; and in grati-

CHILDREN GOING DOWN A MINE LESS THAN A HUNDRED
YEARS AGO.

tude for what he had done for them the
costers of London, when he was an old
man, made him a member of their Union.

As he became known to the poor people
in the slums, he was able to go where others
dared not. He went and talked to burglars;
they all welcomed him; for they knew that
he was really their friend. Many of them
he helped to go overseas and start a new life.

Even the thieves of London loved him;
and here is a story of what once happened
to him. Lord Shaftesbury had a gold watch

which he valued very much, not because it
was gold, but because it had been given to
him by his old nurse whom he loved dearly
when he was a child. One day he went
into the East End of London and had his
watch stolen. This made him very sorrowful.
But two days later there came a ring at the
bell of his house; and when the servant
went and opened the door, he found no
one there, but in the porch lay a sack; and in
the sack was something that moved. When
the sack was opened, inside was found a
small boy bound with rope and gagged; and
round his neck was tied the gold watch,
and with it a scrap of paper, on which was
written, " This is the boy that stole your
watch. You can do what you like with
him." Or, if those were not the very words,
that is what they meant.

Lord Shaftesbury was very glad to have
his watch back again; but he was still more
glad to be given the boy who had stolen it.
He did not punish him, nor get him sent to
prison; he just took care of him himself,
and had him trained so that he could make
his living more honestly.

Not long after Lord Shaftesbury's death,

a new street was being made in London; in his memory it was called Shaftesbury Avenue. At the end of it is Piccadilly Circus; and in the middle of the Circus is a fountain, which is also named after him. On the top of the fountain is a figure of Love, with great wings, flying swiftly, and in his outstretched hand he carries a bow. That figure was made to remind us of the good Lord Shaftesbury, who spent his life in doing service to his fellow men.

A CHILD PULLING A COAL TROLLEY IN A MINE LESS
THAN A HUNDRED YEARS AGO.

THE STORY OF THE ATLANTIC CABLE

1858

I N the year 1858—more than seventy years ago—the first telegraph cable was laid across the bed of the Atlantic Ocean from England to America.

The first proposal for an electric telegraph for sending messages had been made in the days of Wolfe and Clive. Soon men of science were working hard at the idea. Then, a year after Waterloo, a man named Francis Ronalds laid eight miles of wire up and down his garden at Hammersmith; and along the wire he made experiments which seemed to show that, by means of wires, electric messages could be carried any distance. But it was not till some years after Victoria had become Queen that the first telegram from any distance was sent in England.

Then, in due course, men wanted to lay wires under the oceans, from continent to continent, all over the world.

But a mere wire laid under the sea was not

enough. Ropelike lines, containing the wires, were needed, and these we call cables. These cables had to be made of great thickness, with coverings which would not wear out, and would protect the inside wire from the water and so prevent the escape of electricity. And a continuous cable of three thousand miles was hard to make, and also very costly. Then, when it was made, there was the question of how to lay it.

At first, men-of-war were used for carrying the cable; one-half the length of cable required was put on an American ship and started from America, and the other half was put on a British ship and started from Ireland. And as the ships travelled, they ran the cable overboard, letting it sink to the bottom of the sea.

But on the first attempt one of the cables snapped, and the broken end of it was lost and could not be found again. On the second attempt the ships met a great storm in mid-ocean which lasted for nearly a week; and the ships were so strained that they had to return to their starting-point.

The third attempt succeeded. Two ships, a British called the *Agamemnon* and a United States ship called the *Niagara*, each carrying one half of the cable, went out to the middle of the Atlantic; and there, having joined the cable, they parted, one sailing east and the other sailing west, laying out the cable as they went. This time the two ends of the cable reached land safely; one was brought to shore at Valentia in Ireland, and the other in Newfoundland, while from there another length of cable ran on to New York.

England and America were joined at last for the exchange of messages. The first message, one of good wishes and good will, went from Queen Victoria to the President of the United States.

A few years later a big ship called the *Great Eastern* was used for the special purpose of laying a stouter and a stronger cable. But again the cable broke. In 1866, however, the new cable was laid. Today there are no less than fourteen lines across the Atlantic. And going from this and other countries, there are cables lying under the sea in all directions, so that messages can be sent to almost any part of the world, at a speed far greater than the goblin Puck[1] imagined when

[1] Shakespeare, *A Midsummer Night's Dream*, Act II. Scene i, line 175.

H.M.S. "AGAMEMNON" COMPLETING THE FIRST ATLANTIC CABLE AT VALENTIA IN IRELAND.

he boasted he could "put a girdle round about the earth in forty minutes."

Thus modern inventions have brought the peoples of the world much nearer together. The nations know a great deal more of each other than they did in the past. Travel is quicker. The exchange of trade is greater.

And since the discovery of wireless, a voice speaking in Australia can be heard in England, and a voice speaking from England in Australia. Perhaps, in a few years, now that wireless has been discovered, ocean cables may no longer be needed. Today, indeed, we receive accounts of events almost while they are happening on the other side of the globe.

U.S.N.S. "NIAGARA" COMPLETING THE CABLE AT THE AMERICAN END.

THE FIRST FLIGHT ACROSS
THE ATLANTIC

1919

ALL down the centuries the human race
has been travelling about the world.
At first travelling was very slow. There
were no roads; deserts and forests and swamps
lay in the way.

In their small boats men feared to cross
the open sea; they went round by the coast;
and unknown coasts being dangerous, they
often got wrecked. In early days it took men
weeks and months to go distances which now
take only a few hours.

The greater speed at which men now travel
is the result of some of the world's greatest
discoveries. It is going to change history,
for the faster men travel, the smaller the earth
seems to become. All over the world people
of different nations are getting to see each
other more often, and to know each other
better.

Only very gradually has man learned to

make travelling safe. And only in quite modern times has he found means greatly to increase his speed. At first he did it by making roads; then by making better roads, where horses could gallop and coaches run easily.

Then, a hundred years ago or so, railways were invented, and George Stephenson ran his first train. And on the sea steamships began to take the place of sailing vessels. Then ships became bigger and their engines stronger; and the voyage to America, which took Columbus more than three months, can now be made in five days.

But the greatest change of all has come in our own days. Man has learned to fly. The first flights (in December, 1903) were about thirty-five miles an hour—that is, about half as fast as man could travel by steam in a train. In a few years he could fly three or four times as fast as he could go by steam. Today he is able to go longer and longer distances, at greater and greater speed.

In 1919 the first flight was made across the Atlantic between Europe and America, and it took only sixteen hours. That was the first flight across the ocean that was ever made, and here is the story of it.

THE START FROM NEWFOUNDLAND OF THE FIRST FLIGHT
ACROSS THE ATLANTIC.

An English newspaper had offered a prize
of £10,000 to the first man who could fly
from America to Europe within a certain
time. Two airmen, named Brown and Al-
cock, made up their minds to do it. It was
a very dangerous thing to attempt, for nothing
on so big a scale had ever been done before
and very little was known about the high air
currents between Europe and America.

But on June 14th, 1919, these two brave
men, starting from St. John's, Newfoundland,

made the attempt, and did in fact win the prize.

The wind was blowing in the right direction. " If this wind holds," said one of them, " we shall do it in sixteen hours." They had hardly started when they flew into dense fog. Fog above, fog below, they could not see where they were going; they could not even be sure whether they were flying right way up or upside down: for when a flying machine is going at great speed, it flies almost equally well either way.

They had started in the afternoon, at about four o'clock. A strong gale with sleet and hail was blowing. As they mounted into high air it became so cold that everything froze. They sat within the shelter of their machine; but if they tried to look out over the side, the sleet and ice took bits out of their faces. The fog was so thick that they did not know whether they were high up or low down; no horizon could be seen—nothing but mist. This went on for hours. Once, as they came down, they nearly struck the water, and found that they were flying almost upside down. Had they not righted themselves quickly they would have been drowned.

After flying for nearly twelve hours they caught sight of the Pole-star. By this they were able to correct their course and find out in what direction they were going. While one held the steering-wheel the other had to feed him. They ate sandwiches and drank coffee.

Then five hours later they caught sight of the coast of Ireland. They had flown nearly 2,000 miles in less than sixteen hours, at the rate of 122 miles per hour; and flying all through the night and through fog for most of the way, they had kept so good a course that they landed within three miles of the place they had intended.

It was a wonderful thing to have done, and though it has often been done since, that first flight across the Atlantic remains one of the great events in the world's story. And someone put the matter in very simple words: " They had their tea in Newfoundland, and next day they breakfasted in Ireland on ham and eggs."

Less than a hundred years ago it took six months to journey by sea from London to the coast of India; in 1920 it took about three and a half weeks by sea; in 1930, by air, it took about four days.

" IN THIS SIGN, CONQUER !"

1904

A^T the top of a high mountain in South America stands a great figure of Christ holding a cross. It stands on the border between two countries—Chile and Argentina —to tell the world, and all the generations that come after, how they chose peace instead of war.

About the year 1900, these two nations were in fierce dispute. They were quarrel-ling about a certain tract of border land. Each claimed the right to it; and neither would give in.

So they were preparing to settle the matter by going to war.

But it so happened that Argentina had a bishop who, on Easter Day, preached a sermon against war, and said that Christian people should be able to settle their quarrels in a Christian way.

The news of that great sermon was carried across the border, and a bishop of Chile came out and said the same thing. So these two bishops, going from town to town and from village to village, became the voice of peace, each to his own country and people.

At first the men of the two countries would not listen to them; but the women and the priests were more sensible, and backed the bishops up. Presently great numbers of the simple country folk joined them; great meetings were held, asking for peace instead of war.

And now that the two peoples were really set on peace, war could not be made. So the rulers of the two countries decided that a friendly country should settle their quarrel for them.

And the country they chose was Britain. They sent asking Queen Victoria to settle the dispute; and when she died before the task was finished, it was carried on by Edward VII. An agreement between the two countries was made, and the land over which they had quarrelled was divided between them.

Now when this happy result had been reached, the people of those two countries were wise enough to see that, with good will, the same thing could always be done. So they made a treaty of peace which was to last for five years. And since these two neighbours were no longer afraid of each other, they agreed also to reduce the size both of their armies and of their navies.

Now the plan worked so well, not only for the saving of tempers, but for the saving of money also, that at the end of four years they raised up a monument of Peace so placed on the border that both countries might see it. And as the guns of the forts had now become useless, they were removed and melted down, and cast into a great bronze figure of Christ, holding up a Cross—the sign of the Victory of Peace.

As the right place for that statue, they chose the highest point of the mountain range, called the Andes, which forms the border of the two countries—a peak 13,000 feet high. First they carried the statue by train up the mountain-side as far as the railway could go, then on a gun-carriage drawn by mules. And when the mules could go no further, soldiers and sailors from the two countries came with ropes and drew the statue up to the top, where it now stands.

And after the placing of the statue on the

THE CHRIST OF THE ANDES.

pedestal which had been built for it, a day of solemn thanksgiving was ordered.

On both sides of the border the people of the two nations gathered in great numbers to see the statue unveiled, and to pray that what had happened between them, who were once so nearly at war, might happen through all the world.

That is what the League of Nations is working to bring about.

And if the people of the nations which belong to the League will do as did the people of those two countries in South America, then war may end and peace may come.

GENEVA: THE HOME OF THE LEAGUE OF NATIONS

THE MAP-MAKER

THE map of the world is marked with
    lines—
Rivers, and forests, and mountain spines,
Shores of lakes, and edges of coast;
But the marks and lines which cover it most
Are all the cities and roads which man
Has made since work in the world began.
And the bigger the map, the more is seen
How busy a map-maker man has been.

All the places where four roads meet,
Hedges of fields, and crisscross street,
Mountain tracks, with their ups and downs,
Walls, and gates, and towers of towns,
Bridges of rivers, harbours, locks,
Landing-stages, lighthouses, docks,
Churches, palaces, theatres, domes;
Thousands of cities, and millions of homes!

How can one ever complete the list?
Add as you will, there is more you've missed.
Wherever man travels, or builds, or mines,
The map of the world gets covered with lines

Out on the sea is space and to spare—
Up overhead there is space in the air;
And wherever 'tis found — so the mind of
    man wills it—
He plans, and invents, and then makes, till
    he fills it !

O beautiful world, how the hand of man
Has furrowed your face since time began!
And now, if his work be fair and fit,
What is to be the meaning of it?
O man, of the furrowed face you have lined
Now take a little thought, and be kind!
And if of your work you seek increase,
To the power and riches thereof add—peace!